WE'RE GOING
Home

Also from Islandport Press

Moon in Full
Marpheen Chann

The Ghosts of Walter Crockett
W. Edward Crockett

Dear Maine
Morgan Rielly and Reza Jalali

Take It Easy
John Duncan

Whatever It Takes
May Davidson

Hauling by Hand
Dean Lawrence Lunt

This Day in Maine
Joseph Owen

Downeast Genius
Earl Smith

Old Maine Woman
Glenna Johnson Smith

WE'RE GOING
Home

A True Story of Life and Death

Cynthia Thayer

ISLANDPORT PRESS

Islandport Press
P.O. Box 10
Yarmouth, Maine 04096
www.islandportpress.com
info@islandportpress.com

First Printing: November 2023
Printed in the United States of America.
All photographs, unless otherwise noted, courtesy of Cynthia Thayer.

ISBN: 978-1-952143-74-8
Library of Congress Control Number: 2023946781

Dean L. Lunt | Editor-in-Chief, Publisher
Shannon M. Butler | Vice President
Emily A. Lunt | Book Designer
Cover Photo by Ruby Taddeo.

To Art O'Keefe and Becky O'Keefe who, for more than forty-five years, have been our kind, generous, dear friends, and partners in mischief.

TABLE OF CONTENTS

Prologue

I was born in New York City to a beautiful, alcoholic, and fashionable mother and a gay Canadian opera singer father who remained in the closet his whole life. Most of my growing-up years were spent in Nova Scotia, where my father was from. I took piano lessons, ballet lessons, figure-skating lessons, and—the only one of the lessons I loved—horseback riding lessons. I was expected to be the best at everything but I wasn't, except perhaps for the riding. I loved feeling at one with a horse, loved the feel of its body underneath me, powerful and strong. The most memorable moment in my youth was riding the chestnut mare, Cherry Dale, with my Irish mentor, Lettie, beside me on her Arabian hunter. We tossed the saddles and our boots onto the beach and rode the horses into the ocean, bareback and barefoot. The moment the horses began swimming, when their hooves no longer touched sand, I felt like I could do anything and no one could stop me.

My parents did the best they could at making sure we were exposed to the arts and conformed to social norms, but my childhood was dedicated to fighting against being controlled, trying to be myself, but never knowing who that self was. When I met my first husband, he was exotic and was what I wanted at the time—someone my parents wouldn't embrace. But he tried to control me, too. The marriage soured, leaving me with two children—one severely handicapped—to raise myself.

Then some years later, I met Bill. We were an unlikely couple. Bill was older by seven years. He came from a well-to-do family and was an only child. I came from a wannabe well-to-do family and was oldest of four. He was kind and loving, and at first, I thought he might be much too nice for me. I had been a feisty child and had grown into a feisty adult.

Bill grew up in Hingham, Massachusetts, attended Noble and Greenough prep school, promptly flunked out of University of Vermont, and sold life insurance for his father's business. He was successful, had married well, and had three daughters. Life was good until his first wife asked for a divorce. She was in another relationship.

Bill took the plunge and decided to quit the business. He went back to school, where he got his bachelor's and master's degrees in psychology and special education. His life seemed so normal and unusual to me because mine had been so full of strife and lies and alcohol that I thought that was just the way people were. Having loving parents without ever-present tension was foreign to me.

We became the perfect couple, disparate as we seemed. Although we had different styles, we were both Pisces—dreamers, lovers, intuitive, imaginative. We both had the same secret dream that we had never thought possible and had not yet explored. We had a balance of respect and love that made our relationship work. Sometimes I think of that moment in the ocean with Cherry Dale, my clothes soaked with brine, that moment the horse's hooves left the sand beneath us. That moment where I felt no one was controlling me. A feeling that I never felt again.

Until I met Bill.

Chapter 1

MORNING

I wake at 4:05 a.m., my usual time, roll onto my back, and listen for movement from the other room. When Bill began sleeping in the room across the hall in our old farmhouse because I started to snore, I made him promise to come and greet me before he goes downstairs. It's still dark outside but tomorrow will be a wee bit lighter. Every morning, without fail, he slips into our room.

At 4:10 a.m., Bill's alarm squawks. It snaps off immediately. He is already awake. I love listening to him in the stillness of the morning. We have been married forty-five years, and there is intimacy even when I can't see him. I hear him let out a deep breath; some mornings I hear him mumble something softly to himself. The bed creaks when he rises from it. His belt buckle jangles as he pulls on his jeans. Bill puts on the same kind of clothes every day: old jeans, T-shirt with a pocket, plaid flannel shirt, the knitted vest I made him, athletic socks. He leaves his boots downstairs. When I sense he's nearly dressed, I roll over in the bed so I am facing the door and wait.

Bill smiles when he comes in. The light is dim because the sun hasn't risen. However, a weak, pre-dawn light bleeds in from the hallway, and it's enough to let me see him smiling.

"How did you sleep?" he asks.

"Okay," I say. "I heard you get up to pee a couple of times."

He raises his hand and I know what he's going to do. His fingers, swollen from arthritis, form the American Sign Language sign for "I love you." I return the gesture. It's our morning ritual. He bends over me and his lips touch my forehead. Not really a kiss. Just a light touch to remind me that we love each other and will always respect each other. I don't know what love means to others, but to me it means Bill's touch against my forehead before the sun rises.

He leaves our room, holds the banister, and goes slowly down our steep stairs, foot by foot. The first thing he does is start fires in both the drum-room stove and the old cook stove in the kitchen. It's mid-March so we still need both stoves going. The cast iron plates on the cook stove clatter as he settles the logs under them. Then it's quiet and I strain to hear the subtle but familiar sounds of Bill doing his back exercises in the room where he keeps his drums. I can tell which exercise he's doing by the sounds he makes: swish, he's lying down and grabbing one knee after the other; thud, he lifts his leg up and drops it onto the rug; then, no sound, as he does his push-ups and sit-ups. About twenty-five years ago, Bill's doctor gave him the set of exercises to do after a back episode and he's done them every morning without fail. Bill is a man who embraces routine.

I know he's putting on his boots because I hear one thud on the kitchen floor. He checks his email, lets our dog Kelpie out of her hut, and takes her for a short walk. The hut is really just a standard wire dog crate, but Bill and I think *hut* sounds better than *cage*. When he comes back in, I hear him whack the dog's stainless bowl against the side of the woodstove and I hear the dog's nails clicking as she does her little before-breakfast-prance in praise of food before she races into her hut and sits while Bill fills her bowl.

"There you go," he says. And I hear him shut the latch on Kelpie's hut.

After Bill feeds Kelpie, I don't hear much, but some kitchen smells drift upstairs and I know he's making himself toast and scrambled eggs before he goes out to do the animal chores. One thing I love about staying in bed later than Bill is that by the time I get up, the house is toasty warm. If something happened to him, I'd have to get up in the cold and light the stoves myself.

I hear the door open, then close firmly. He and our farming partner Shepsi, along with our apprentice, feed the horses, the sheep, and the chickens. They put the horses out back and let the laying hens into the yard. He slams the door of his green pickup truck and starts the engine. That's my signal to get out of bed. He'll be gone about a half hour.

By the time he returns from Young's Store with his coffee full of milk and sugar, and a copy of the *Bangor Daily News*, I've heated water for my tea, checked my email, taken care of any Airbnb messages, and anything else that's worth responding to. Then I go out to the kitchen to get the news and the gossip— mostly gossip.

"Anything new?" I ask. It's the same thing every morning.

"It's going to be a beautiful day," Bill says, tossing the paper on the table and kicking off his insulated rubber boots. "Lobstermen are all out." He replaces his boots with a very old pair of dilapidated leather workboots with no laces, which he calls his "slippers." He is deliberate and slow. I am frantic and fast.

I'm a bit preoccupied. I'm excited because tonight's the first rehearsal for our local production of Neil Simon's *Lost in Yonkers*, which I am directing. I'm excited.

"Going to the woods to haul out a couple of logs," Bill says, unfolding the newspaper onto the table. "I want to get them out before all the snow melts." We read the newspaper in tandem. It's my favorite part of the day. A sort of newspaper pas de deux. We sit side by side and, without a word, pass the sections back and forth to each other—there is intimacy in our silence.

I sip my tea and Bill gulps his coffee from his chipped travel mug. I'm not really hungry yet so I start the crossword. "Staving off Alzheimer's," I tell Bill. It's Thursday so the crossword is getting harder. I probably won't finish it. It's much more likely I'll finish the puzzle on a Monday or a Tuesday because they start off easy and get progressively more difficult as the week goes on. I'm a casual crossword enthusiast. It makes Bill chuckle.

After breakfast, he goes out to the barn to get his horses ready for the woods. I go to my office in the back of the house to work on edits I'm doing on a draft of a student's novel-in-progress. I love writing, but like many writers I almost love editing more. It's a thrill to be able to take a piece of writing, mine or someone else's, and add or subtract something from it that makes it more alive, more true, than it was before I put my red pen to it.

I put my feet up on the couch in my office, call Kelpie to join me, and pull the novel manuscript onto my lap. The morning passes quickly. At some point, Bill comes in and says he's made good progress hauling wood and is taking a breather.

"The ice is starting to break up. I'll finish this afternoon."

Then he's gone again, out the door. Every day, Bill goes somewhere for what I call his "toot." Usually it's to Milbridge, the next town up the coast, to make a deposit at the bank or to the grocery for something or other. Sometimes he just drives around town to see what's happening or check in at the town hall. He's one of the town's five selectmen. He comes back before lunchtime and I hear pans clanging in the kitchen. When I finish my chapter, I go to join him.

Bill stands at our big restaurant-grade gas stove. I see why he went to the grocery. Hot dogs. He's trying to hide them but I can see the open package on the counter. He's got the big cast iron frying pan smoking. We have a long-running joke that he's only allowed to have two hot dogs on July Fourth and it's only March 14. He knows they aren't good for him and that I don't approve, but I laugh. It's kind of embarrassing that an organic farmer would eat hot dogs for lunch, but it doesn't happen very often. Maybe it's July Fourth somewhere in the universe.

"Ohhhhh," I tease, "the red ones, eh?" I think Maine is the only state that sells bright red hot dogs. Bill's spread all the accouterments—rolls, French's mustard, chopped onions, and relish from our root cellar—on the island counter, but no plate. He puts two dogs and two rolls in the sizzling pan, then turns and smiles at me as if to say, "See? I'm having hot dogs." It's his mischievous smile. I smile back. He uses his linen napkin to carry the hot dogs to the table.

"It's okay," I say. "Two?"

"Only two."

I grab some leftover chicken wings, from chicken we raised, from the fridge and take them into my office so I can pick and nibble while I continue working on the edits. Bill takes a short nap in his chair, which is a real skill, one I've never mastered. He just sits down and he's asleep, snoring softly. He wakes up about fifteen minutes later, refreshed and ready to work. After his power nap he putters around. Early afternoon, he opens my office door to tell me he's going back to the woods but he won't be long. "Only a couple of logs that I want to bring in. Not much time left in the woods," he says.

"We'll have to eat early," I say. "I have rehearsal. First one."

"I'll probably be back before you go. If I'm not, break a leg." And off he goes.

Bill loves working the horses in the woods when the snow is slick and the logs slide noiselessly, attached to his red two-wheeled logging arch. For more than forty years, he's been working our woodlot across the street from the farm, harvesting saw logs, pulp wood, and plenty of firewood to heat our leaky old farmhouse, leaving the woodlot in better and better shape each year. Sometimes Bill stands up in the logging arch like a chariot driver in the movies, calling out orders to the horses. I wish he wouldn't stand. I tell him it isn't safe to stand, but what's the point? He knows that, and yet he does it anyway. Just as he loves his rhythms and routines, Bill does what he wants. So do I. That's one of the few ways we are the same.

The novel I'm editing came from a writer who attended a presentation I gave last month in Portland for Maine Writers & Publishers Alliance. The writing is pulling me in, though it has some pacing problems. I love the characters but I mark it up when I see something that stops the story. I sip my cool tea left over from the morning as I flip back and forth between my editor and theater director's hats. Both the roles of an editor and a director excite me, but sometimes they get in each other's way. I decide to go with the director's hat for the rest of the afternoon because the first rehearsal is tonight. With a clipboard on my lap, I take notes on chartreuse card stock. As in life, in theater and in fiction, it's not what the character says or does, but why a character says or does something that is the most important thing.

I'm so focused on my work that I only half hear someone bursting through the kitchen door and rushing down the hall toward my office. "Cynthia, you in there?"

I don't answer, but Shepsi keeps coming. He stops at the doorway. "Bill's in the middle of the road," he blurts. "I think he's alive." Then he turns quickly and leaves, as if I am to follow him.

"Okay, I'll be out in a minute," I say, staring at my stack of card stock. I'm almost finished with the motivation list for tonight, I think. Just a few more minutes.

Then I realize what Shepsi said. *Bill's in the middle of the road. I think he's alive.*

I toss my clipboard and notes onto the floor and rush out the door, almost tripping on the threshold. *I think he's alive.* That means he might not be. "What?" I yell. But Shepsi's already in the kitchen. Then I hear the door close.

Chapter 2

In The Beginning

Ever since Bill and I met in 1973 in graduate school back in Massachusetts, my world got better. We were both divorced, had children—five altogether—and were untraditional students at Bridgewater State University, as it's called now. After my divorce, I had made a bad choice in men, which I was just beginning to realize. I needed to get out of the toxic relationship, but I was afraid to, for whatever reason.

Bill was living in a little house behind a Unitarian Universalist Church in West Bridgewater, Massachusetts, where Reverend Rich, a very politically outspoken minister, held court. Bill and I were both anti–Vietnam War protestors and I first noticed him when my brother Bob, who was visiting from Canada, and I went to one of Rich's Sunday services out of curiosity. Bob started campaigning for Bill but I was cautious. Not really my type.

"Who is that?" Bob asked.

"I think his name is Bill," I said. "I saw him at an encounter group at the college. He lives in back of the church."

"Very cute," Bob said.

Bill had a bushy red beard that grew halfway down his chest and a shiny bald head, which I found a fascinating combination—he wasn't swarthy at all. He was tall and thin—not really my type. And I was still in a relationship that I knew wasn't the healthiest. So when my brother suggested we ask Bill to a play in Boston, instead of the guy I was backing away from, I said, "I think he's too nice for me."

But we found Bill and went to dinner before a brilliant performance of *One Flew Over the Cuckoo's Nest*, a book that I had been teaching to my high school seniors and that I loved. I found the characters incredibly well developed. Chief was always my favorite, but even though Nurse Ratched was a nasty piece of work, I loved her character. Bill was quiet, but when he spoke, he had something to say. I found myself relaxing with him, moving closer to him so that our arms were touching. Yes, he was nice.

Bill told me later that he drove by my apartment once and said to his girls, "The woman I'm going to marry lives there."

We saw each other at the college and soon after the initial meeting for dinner and the play, I spent the night at his little apartment behind the church. And so it began.

We had a great summer with his three girls and my two children—Tom and Robin, who is deaf and multiply handicapped. We went canoeing, camping, picnicking, had dinner with our dear friends, the Coles, and Bill moved into my sweet little apartment. I adored him. He was kind and thoughtful, something I wasn't used to. And there was something about his smell that was new and refreshing. I loved his freckles and his silliness. And he was an amazing father to his three girls.

His daughters, Sara, Amy, and Alison, lived with his ex-wife not far away in the town of Hingham, and we saw them often. Bill called them every night without fail to chat about their day or to make plans for the weekend.

We talked about getting married and decided to have a small wedding at the UU Church and to do it before the end of the year. I was teaching high school at the time and could be fired for living with someone without the "benefit" of wedlock. All teachers

Me in my twenty-dollar Indian dress and Bill wearing an embroidered shirt on our wedding day December 29, 1973 when my hair was brown and his was red.

had to sign a contract stating that we were not committing "moral turpitude," so Bill and I set a date of December 29, 1974.

I didn't want to make another mistake. My first marriage had been a disaster and ended in a contentious divorce. I spent many hours trying to figure out what the main reason was. There were many. He was lazy. I was stubborn. He was selfish. I was stubborn. He couldn't hold a job. I was stubborn. But it wasn't just stubbornness. All my life, people, starting with my parents, teenage relationships, my first husband, and then my "bad relationship boyfriend," had told me what to do. I always thought life would be great if people would just stop telling me what to do. Could it be that simple?

I remember clearly the moment when I mentioned it to Bill. We were up earlier than the kids and were having a quiet cup of coffee at the picnic table we had set up in the living room. It was the day before the wedding.

"Bill," I said. "There's something important I have to say."

"What is it, Dolly?" he said. Bill had many nicknames for me but this was my favorite, and he knew that.

"Please don't ever tell me what to do."

"Wouldn't think of it."

We both had teaching jobs; Bill taught middle-school special ed and I taught twelfth grade English and theater. The apartment I was renting wasn't really big enough for seven people, so we bought an old run-down Cape Cod house nearby. We discovered it was really a treasure. It had been built in 1715 and much of the original work had been covered up and preserved. Ugly cardboard hid the wide board paneling in the two main rooms. When we ripped off old wallboard in the kitchen, we found a period fireplace—surprise! An extension had been built out the back many years before and, when we tore off the siding, underneath were the original shingles from 1715. A history class from the university came to look at the wall because it was so unusual.

We worked hard for those two years, teaching, plowing up ground for a garden, learning to milk goats, and most of all, restoring the old house to as close to its original as possible. Then we got a call from Bill's ex, saying she was moving to Maine with the children. We made an almost instant decision. We put the house on the market, gave notice at our teaching jobs, sold the house for a hefty profit thanks to an ad in the *New York Times* and started looking at property in Maine.

A few months after Bill's ex moved, we followed, kit and caboodle, to the northeast coast of Maine, with kids, ponies, sheep, chickens, and goats in tow. It was our dream, although we weren't even aware of it until the opportunity to pursue it came up.

We found an old farmhouse and barn with a path leading down to a pink granite shore in *Yankee* after looking at many places that were too big, too small, not in the right town, too close to the road, no barn. The first time we drove up the driveway guarded by a very old dead pine that was riddled with woodpecker holes, I knew I had to live here. Gouldsboro. A small fishing village on the coast of Maine, populated with strong men and women who love the sea and were ruled by it.

The driveway was long and meandering, with a grassy path growing tall up the middle. At the top of the hill was a ramshackle old gray house across from a huge barn covered in ugly pink shingles. The kitchen wainscoting was painted fluorescent yellow and the plaster above the chair rail was a disgusting orangey brown, crisscrossed by white lines where someone had attempted to seal cracks in the horsehair plaster. On the floor was scuffed and worn beige print linoleum, curling at the edges. The sink, obviously built for someone four feet tall, operated by a foot pump to bring water from the basement cistern into the sink, and the water in the cellar was almost knee deep. And the bathroom walls were covered with grotesque pink plastic tiles.

When we arrived with our rented moving van and entourage of children and animals, we settled the ponies and sheep and chickens into the barn. When everything was taken care of and the kids were in bed, we shared a bottle of wine. It was then I realized that in the two years we had been together, he had never once told me what to do. That's why we got along so well.

"I love it here," I said.

"Me, too.

"I feel like I can be myself, wear crappy clothes if I want."

"I'm getting rid of my suits," Bill said. "All of them."

"We did it," I said. "Didn't we?"

Bill raised his glass, smiled like only he can, and said, "We surely did, Dolly."

Chapter 3

THE WILD RIDE TO THE HOSPITAL

I follow Shepsi out the kitchen door. Outside, he turns to me. "I'll take you down there," he says. We get into my little red car.

On the way down our driveway, Shepsi tells me he was ground driving Archie, one of our Haflinger horses, to join Bill in the woods. At the bottom of the driveway, he saw fire engines and police cars with lights flashing. A group of people were clustered around something in the road that he thought at first was a bunch of rags. Then he realized it was Bill. He turned Archie around and rushed back up the driveway to tell me. He doesn't know anything other than that, he says. I notice the driveway is edged with small snowbanks that are beginning to melt.

I think, *He's got to be fine. Probably took a tumble and landed in the road. He's lucky someone didn't run over him.* I sit back, relax a little as we get close to the old dead pine at the end of the driveway. Besides, it could actually be a bunch of rags or the carcass of a deer that got hit by a car. Or Kelpie. But Kelpie's in the kitchen.

Two ambulances are there, lights flashing, as Shepsi pulls as close to the huddled group as he can before stopping to let me out. I hurry toward them, beginning to feel panic. I rarely panic.

In a way, I want to slow down, not get there too quickly. I hesitate. The heap is right on the faded yellow centerline a few car-lengths from our driveway entrance. How did all these people and vehicles get here so quickly and I didn't know anything about it? It seems Bill left minutes ago saying he was going to the woods. It couldn't have been more than fifteen minutes. It couldn't.

I reach the group gathered around and look down. It is indeed Bill. And he is indeed alive, his orange watch cap at an odd angle. He's flailing his arms in the air, struggling against the ambulance team trying to get him onto the gurney. "Bill, please let them help you," I say. "You need to go to the hospital."

"Horses," he says, staring at me with one pleading eye. The other is bulging like there's a golf ball beneath his eyelid. He's terrified. I've never seen him terrified. I guide him to the gurney, help them lift his legs in place, but he's agitated, fights against me, looks around for his horses. I have no idea where they are but I don't tell him that. Perhaps they're still in the woods.

"They'll be fine," I say. "I promise you. I'll bring them home." His swollen eye is unsettling and I almost laugh out loud. It's so enormously distended it seems he has only one eye—the huge one. His other eye is small, insignificant against the cyclops one. His sweatshirt hood falls back. There is only a scratch on his bald head. And his glasses are gone.

We manage to get him loaded onto the gurney and the EMTs and firefighters lift him into the waiting town ambulance. I know the people. Many of them fish for lobsters and are finished hauling for the day. The people are tough here on the coast of Maine, most living an honest hardworking existence near the sea, which tempers them but makes them resilient and independent. Aaron, from next door, who cuts firewood for a living; Tate, the fire chief, whose brother, Jim, is one of Bill's best friends; and others I recognize from town. They have serious expressions on their faces. Everyone in town knows Bill because he's been a selectman

Bill with the horses, Star and Andy. They were acquired after the fire killed our other horses. Bill's first thought after his accident was of their safety.

for years. And everyone loves him. Even the hardscrabble yahoos who cause havoc around town love him. This news will be all over town by dark.

"Here they come," someone yells. I hear panic in the voice but I'm not sure whose voice it is. I look down the road toward the highway, and the horses, normally calm and relaxed, are galloping toward us, nostrils flared, ears back, red logging arch bouncing and banging on its two wheels like a Roman racing chariot behind them, its seat empty. They must have turned around before they got to the main highway. I step out in front of them, spread my arms wide. They'll stop for me.

"Whoa," I say. "Stop." They keep coming. "Whoa," I say again. I jump out of the way just before they're about to run me down. "Star. Andy. Whoa!"

They always stop on a dime when they hear the word "Whoa." Bill trained them well. I turn, watch them race toward our driveway, the logging arch fishtailing back and forth. I've never seen them run like this. They're workhorses, slow and steady. The people in the road back away in fear as Star and Andy gallop faster and faster. When they get to the driveway, they swerve, the arch swinging out, and charge up the driveway, toward the barn, toward their safe stalls where nothing bad can happen to them.

Shepsi turns my car around and follows them. He'll make sure they go into their stalls and quiet them down.

Bill's only word had been, "Horses . . ." I'm torn for a moment between going after them, which is what he would want, or staying with him. It's an easy choice. Shepsi will take care of everything. I hurry toward the waiting ambulance. "I'm coming with him."

"We've called for a LifeFlight helicopter. We'll meet it down the road. Get in."

I see Liz, Shepsi's partner, pull up behind the ambulance in my little red car. Shepsi must have the kids. And the horses. It's foggy, late afternoon. It's a movie. I truly think it is. Part of me knows it's real but a bigger part of me thinks it's a movie. Like a dream. A Fellini film.

I climb up into the cab of the ambulance. I have nothing with me except for the few things I grabbed when I ran from the house. No jacket. No hat. No phone.

Sitting in the ambulance, I realize I won't be back in the house that night. I should have grabbed my iPad. I have no way

to contact anyone. The other vehicles stand down, turn off their
blinking lights, and leave for their homes in Winter Harbor and
Prospect Harbor and Corea, to stoke their stoves and have supper
with their families. Then I see my little red car behind us. It's Liz,
waiting. She's coming, too.

Bill is laid out on a gurney in the back with an attendant
fussing over him. He's agitated. They give him something to calm
him down. I have no idea what it is but he quickly calms and
stops flailing. I speak to him quietly. "We're going to the hospital.
The horses went home. They're going to be fine. Shepsi's taking
care of them." That seems to soothe him.

We move down the road in an eerie silence. The siren isn't on.
Why isn't it? Maybe they only turn it on when there is traffic, and
the roads here are nearly empty this time of year, this time of day.

Directions about the LifeFlight helicopter crackle from the
CB radio: "Stop at the next field." And we slow down, waiting for
word about the helicopter. Nothing. We wait for a few minutes
and then continue down the road to the next open space. I turn
every few seconds to look at Bill. He's resting. But the bulging
eye hasn't changed. His other eye is closed. Still no helicopter.
We continue onto Route 1 waiting for more directions. The
LifeFlight dispatcher radios in to say that the fog is too thick here
on the coast; we can't fly.

"Where are we going?" I ask.

"Still trying to meet up with the bird."

"Bangor?"

"That's the plan."

We continue to drive. I look back. "Bill?" There's no response
but the attendant assures me that he's been sedated so that he
doesn't hurt himself. That's funny: he's already hurt himself.

"Is Liz behind us?" I ask.

"A little red car?"

"That's it."

"Looks like it," he says.

"What about the chopper?"

"We're still trying to hook up with LifeFlight."

What the fuck happened? Did Bill fall off the logging arch? The ambulance is almost in Ellsworth now, a half-hour's drive from our farm.

"We're stopping at Maine Coast," the driver says. "They'll stabilize him. Then we'll go on to Bangor from there."

Why are we going so slowly? It must be the fog. This is an emergency. They should be going faster. I try to gather myself. I need to be alert. I have a job to do. When I turn back to check on Bill, he looks almost peaceful. He looks like he's taking a nap.

"How is he?" I ask the ambulance attendant.

"Still alive," he says.

Chapter 4

LIFE ON THE FARM

Our first few years in Gouldsboro were spent learning how
to do what we were already doing. And that never stopped. I had
some money in my teacher's retirement fund, which I took out
early to buy a spinning wheel and a weaving loom. We bought
hoes and cultivators and dibbles. It was September and we were
concerned about winter coming. The leaky old farmhouse had
no furnace. We wilted trees, cut them when they were still
covered with leaves and allowed the leaves to pull moisture out
of the wood—the lazy person's way to turn green wood into dry
seasoned logs. Bill bagged a deer the first day of hunting season so
our freezer was full of meat for the winter. Not bad for a couple
of city folks. We knew it would be freezing if we didn't do some
winterization so we blew in cellulose insulation and got combination storm windows installed. It was still freezing.

We named the farm Darthia Farm. Everyone wants to know
where the name came from. Mostly I just say, "Oh, we made
it up. We thought it sounded nice." But the truth is that it's a
combination of Darling and Thia, nicknames Bill used for me if
he didn't call me Dolly.

Bill grew up in just south of Boston, an only child whose
blue-blooded parents sent him to prep school and expected him
to go to Harvard like his dad. I grew up in Nova Scotia, oldest

of four children and taught that working in the dirt with one's hands was only for the lower class. Not the best childhoods to learn how to live the simple country life. We both always felt we were misfits, not really embracing our families' ways.

When we couldn't be outside digging postholes by hand and clearing brush, we pored over farming books and I practiced my spinning and weaving and began to sell coats and jackets with yarn I dyed, wove, and made into clothing. I'd always loved working with my hands—knitting, making mud pies, groveling in the dirt—so the work we were doing was perfect and I loved all of it. I painted and papered all ten rooms of the leaky old farmhouse, finally getting rid of the bright-yellow walls and orangey brown plaster in the kitchen. We redid the bathroom and got rid of the horrendous pink plastic tiles. I was happiest covered in spattered paint or caked with mud. We knocked out one of the kitchen walls to enlarge the cooking area and give us a better height for the sink. Robin went to Governor Baxter School for the Deaf but helped on weekends and Tom went to the local school. Tom was a great help, especially with heavy work. And on weekends, Bill's kids and loads of friends came over and sometimes we even got them to help.

We loved our chosen home. We worked hard and played hard. In just a few years, we had renovated the farmhouse and cleared a lot of land for garden and pasture space. I was selling my woven clothing at fairs all over New England and in the local craft co-op. Bill cut and sold pulp wood and learned to work with horses. Every winter morning for years and years, when snow was on the ground, he'd leave by 8:30 for the woodlot across the street with the horses, his chain saw, a good hearty lunch in his backpack, and sometimes with an interested apprentice. He'd come back around 3 p.m. ready to do the animal chores and get ready for milking. We cut trees, limbed them, and burned the brush, bred goats and cows for milk, made cheese and butter and yogurt, cleared land for gardens and pastures.

It wasn't all work, though. We got everyone except for Robin, our handicapped daughter, cross-country skis and cut trails through the woods across the street. Amy, Alison, Sara, Tom, Bill, and I skied over the woods roads watching for deer or rabbits, loving the *whoosh whoosh* sound of our waxed skis on new snow. Bill's three girls came almost every weekend, bringing their friends. Often there would be close to ten teenagers staying overnight, including our own.

One late winter weekend just as the ice flows were breaking up, the house was full. My son, Tom, and four of his friends, went off exploring before dinner and were gone a long time. Finally the phone rang and it was Tom calling to say they were in Corea and needed a ride.

"How did you get to Corea?" I asked. "Where are you?"

We drove the twenty minutes around the bay to the small fishing village to pick them up and found them soggy wet and shivering. They had all piled onto an ice floe that was frozen into the beach down at our shore. Being boys and brave and all that, they jumped up and down on the floe until it broke off from the shore and began to drift out into the bay. As they floated out toward the open ocean, the ice melted and shrank. Pure luck landed them on a spit of stony outcropping where they could get off and try to find help. If they hadn't, it would have been the end of all of them.

Chapter 5

THE ELLSWORTH HOSPITAL STOP

We pull up to the big glowing red EMERGENCY sign. Volunteer attendants lift Bill out of the ambulance onto the gurney. He's very weak and he isn't moving. But then he wiggles his hand. Is it the "I love you" sign? No. I don't think it is.

Liz parks my car and follows us in where the hospital people tell us to have a seat in the waiting room. They'll call us when we can come in. We sit on uncomfortable chairs in the gloomy room and wait. It seems they are taking too long. We check and check and check.

"Can we come in yet?"

Finally, they send for us. We're led to an emergency room and find him under a thin blue blanket. He looks small in the big adjustable hospital bed. They've undressed him and put him in a johnny; his clothes, that same old outfit he puts on day after day, spill from a paper grocery bag on the floor. His cyclops eye seems even bigger than it had been. I take his hand.

"Bill, you've had an accident. Do you know what happened?"

He looks at me with his little eye and I can tell he has no idea.

Someone comes in with a cervical collar. "We need to put this on in case he's injured his neck," he says. Nurses are pulling his johnny up and sticking heart monitor tags on his chest. He tugs at the collar, trying to take it off.

"You need to keep it on," I say.

"Off," he says.

That's a good sign? That he spoke? Isn't it?

The room is full of nurses, doctors, and technicians, taking X-rays right in the room, checking his blood pressure, reading the heart display, and trying to keep Bill from pulling off the collar. He looks at me and shrugs his shoulders as if to say, "What the fuck is going on?" It's frantic in the room. He stares at me through his good eye, begging to know why he has a collar around his neck. It's as if the collar means he has lost control of himself and now someone else is in charge. And that's true.

I glance at the paper bag on the floor. It's overflowing with his jeans, sweatshirt, red plaid flannel shirt, and tall insulated rubber boots. On top is the knitted vest I made him last fall. He wears it every day. I spun the yarn from our sheep, dyed it with indigo from our garden and cochineal that I got from an organic bug farmer in Central America, and then knitted it to Bill's specs. I often strike out with gifts for him but this was a hit. And then I see what's happened to it. The medics must have slashed a jagged line right up the center of the front, bits of yarn fraying in the air. Who cares at this point? Yet something inside me weeps.

They wheel him out of the crowded room for a CT scan of his head and neck. They want to be sure there are no serious injuries that could cause paralysis. Liz and I take the time to call some people on her phone. I call my son, Tom, and two of Bill's girls, Sara and Amy, to tell them that their dad has had a bad accident and that we will be on the way to Bangor in the helicopter as soon as they stabilize him. What does "stabilize" even mean, I wonder, as I speak to the kids. When he's out of danger? When he doesn't need the collar? When he can walk to the ambulance? They're all upset. I leave it to them to tell Bill's estranged daughter, Alison. She deserves to know what's going on. Robin doesn't need to know yet. I decide to wait until I have something positive to tell her. Robin's deafness is why we know rudimentary American Sign Language and use the I Love You sign.

Then I remember the theater rehearsal. Cathy, my lead actor, is the one to notify but I don't have her number. And I can't send an email because I don't have my iPad. We make more frantic calls to tell people we're about to leave for Bangor in a helicopter. We're stalled here in the Ellsworth hospital emergency room, Northern Lights Maine Coast Memorial Hospital to be exact, and I don't think we're going anywhere soon.

Bill comes back from the CT scan, still grabbing at the hated collar. He hasn't spoken except for saying "Horses . . ." when he was lying in the road, and "Off" when they put the neck collar on him. I plead silently for him to say just one word. Anything would do. "Dolly" would be fantastic, but even another "off" would make me really hopeful, but he doesn't say another word. When I squeeze his hand, he squeezes back and looks at me with his small eye. I feel like he's in there but can't get out, trapped in a body that doesn't work.

Hospital personnel hurry in and out of the small room, checking machines, asking him to squeeze their hands. I tell him he was in an accident over and over but I'm not sure he understands. His eye shows his fear, but I don't know what he is more afraid of: what has happened or what is to come. Afraid of what happened to the horses. Afraid he doesn't know who he is. Afraid of dying. Afraid of being incapacitated. Yes. That's it. He doesn't want to sit on the porch drooling while someone else works his beloved horses in front of him.

When he becomes angry and tries to remove the collar again, the medical team refers to him as combative. I tell them that he's the most patient man I know and it's not like him to be combative. I've never seen him angry like this. And no, he doesn't do drugs. "The real Bill is in there somewhere," I say. But I'm not sure it's true.

I watch his blood pressure monitor and it's steady at one-twenty-six over seventy-eight. Perfect. His pulse is eighty-six. Strong. His respiration is twenty. Normal. It's the blood. The doctors say the CT scan shows a lot of blood oozing through the inside of his brain and leaking into the space between his brain and his skull. He shakes his head "no" when they ask him if he has pain. I wonder how that could be, given the huge swelling on his eye. The minor scrape on his head is the only thing that seems new except for the eye. The doctors keep saying he was kicked in the head by a horse, so I point out that if that were the case, he'd have deep gashes on his head and a broken skull from the sharp caulks he welded onto their iron shoes to give them traction in the snow.

The chaos continues. Children and friends call for updates, people push in and out of the cramped room, Bill pulls at the neck collar. Finally someone comes to report that it's still too foggy to land the helicopter and they'll transport him by ambulance to Bangor, where there is a neurosurgeon waiting. They might operate to relieve pressure caused by all the blood.

Before the move to Bangor, the doctors decide to insert a breathing tube to protect his airway. "He's stable but critical," a doctor tells me. I'm not even sure what that means. And where has he gone? I don't feel his presence anymore.

"What does the CT scan show?" I ask. "I mean besides the lack of cervical damage and the bleeding?"

The doctor says he has both subdural and subarachnoid hemorrhages involving the right and left frontal and parietal lobes.

"Holy crap!" I blurt. "What does that mean? I want to know before we leave for Bangor. What are we dealing with?"

He tells me what I already know about the bleeding. "We'll know more when we get to Bangor. He must have been kicked pretty hard. We're ready to go."

"I'll go with him," I say.

They get him on the gurney to transport him to the ambulance. I glance over at the crumpled paper bag and there's the vest, its frayed ends hanging over the edge. Liz takes the bag, puts it in my car, and follows us.

Bill has been sedated so he doesn't thrash or try to remove the collar. He seems comfortable. I try to relax, watch cars go by. It's beginning to get dark. Bangor is another half hour away but it seems to be taking forever to drive the distance. A few cars pass us, although we're an ambulance. I keep looking at my watch and then back at him to see if he's still breathing.

We get to Brewer and drive along the strip of fast food restaurants and mattress stores. We're almost there. When we pass over the bridge into Bangor, I feel a bit of relief because soon someone will find out what's happening and maybe they can fix it.

"Lots of fog," I say to the ambulance driver. "Not too much traffic."

I make this sort of ridiculous small talk with the ambulance driver while medicated Bill—my Farmer Billy—lies so still in the back.

Chapter 6

BUILDING A FARM

Those first years on the farm were full of hard physical work and making new friends. We woke at 5 a.m. to milk seven goats and, some years later, two cows, had a fast breakfast, worked all day with twenty minutes off for a quick lunch, then at 5 p.m. milking again and did animal chores. The grassy hump up the middle of the driveway slowly disappeared because of the pony and automobile traffic. Where there had been scrub bushes and small trees was now open land, limed, tilled, and seeded to make pasture for the sheep and goats. Many nights we fell into bed still covered with the caked soil from newly made gardens.

But the meals were glorious. For the first time, I was cooking almost exclusively with food we had raised. Chickens we raised and slaughtered ourselves, tomatoes that tasted nothing like a tomato I had ever had, fat carrots and beets, butter and yogurt made from our goats' milk. I've always loved cooking but this was nirvana. What we didn't grow, we got at the local food co-op delivery about once a month and all the neighbors pitched in to divvy up.

I had learned to spin and weave the wool we sheared from our small flock of Dorset sheep. Bill trained three small Shetland ponies until they could plow, haul wood, spread manure, and pull a wagon.

In Maine, some folks say, "Just because a cat has kittens in the oven, doesn't make them biscuits." In other words, you can't really be a Mainer unless your ancestors were born here. But Bill and I were welcomed into the Schoodic Peninsula community, I believe because we worked hard and seemed honest. We always waved, nodded to everyone we passed. On the Maine coast, when you pass another car or truck, you just raise your hand with a small nod and the other driver does the same. No real waving.

We became involved in the running of the community. I became the president of the Schoodic Chamber of Commerce and a Maine Organic Farmers and Gardeners Association (MOFGA) board member. Bill was voted onto the board of the Hancock County Soil and Water Conservation District and eventually became a Gouldsboro Town Selectman.

And I became a Wednesday Spinner. Every Wednesday I packed my car with my spinning wheel and some fleece that I had washed and carded and drove to one of the other spinners' houses. Sometimes it was close by. Sometimes an hour away. Up to twenty of us gathered from mid-morning to mid-afternoon and spun yarn, had marvelous soups, and talked about our lives, our families, and what we were going to do with the yarn we were spinning.

Bill and I bought a couple of head of beef cattle that seemed to get out of the fences with great ease, which kept us occupied. We grafted and planted apple trees but many of them died. We lost one of our Dorset sheep to fly-strike, an awful way to go. We didn't know what we were dealing with until it was too late for one of them, but we stayed up until after midnight with flashlights, scraping maggots off the back of the second one and by some miracle, saved her. We learned, making mistakes along the way.

One of the best things about our move to Downeast coastal Maine was that we could wear exactly what we wanted to wear.

Bill gave away all his clothes except for his jeans, T-shirts, plaid flannel shirts, and green sweatshirts. Around here you can wear what you want. You can go to the opera in Bangor wearing work boots and jeans or go to a contra dance wearing a tuxedo or long dress. We were both nonconformists and loved that we weren't judged for our clothing.

The kids adjusted to country life, although sometimes they missed Massachusetts and their lives there. Tom became a great cross-country runner and practiced running in his bare feet through the woods. Bill's girls joined the theater at their high school in Blue Hill and loved entering a world of *Fiddler on the Roof.* Amy got a riding horse that was more her size than little four-hundred-pound Willow. Robin stayed all week at the Baxter School for the Deaf in Falmouth, near Portland, and came home on weekends.

We got a border collie named Meg who was as weird as a three-dollar bill. Bill trained her to attack a large rubber boot we kept behind the living room stove when he said the words "Ronald Reagan" or "James Watt" or "budget cuts," much to the delight of almost everyone. Meg would race over to the old boot, pick it up in her teeth, and shake it so hard the room vibrated, drop it back where it had been, and lie down at my feet, waiting for the next command.

It was inexpensive entertainment and soon word got around that we had this amazing political dog. Bill loved to show people her tricks with the boot.

And here we were. Living The Good Life.

Chapter 7

BANGOR ICU

The ride into Bangor is interminable. Fog grows thicker
and thicker, keeping the ambulance slow. I chat absurdly, anything to fill the deathly silence broken only by the sound of the
ambulance's strong engine. We finally arrive at the emergency
room at the Bangor hospital and I feel like I'm entering a kind of
brightly lit detention center. When they ask for my ID I feel like
a criminal. And I'm angry at them for taking valuable time from
Bill's care.

When they finally let us go in, we make our way alongside his
gurney to the emergency room where a surgical team awaits him.
Again, a nurse asks me, and Liz, who has followed us, to step into
the waiting room while they look him over. I lean down and tell
him we're going to be close by, but I think he's too sedated to care.

The waiting room smells sour, of rotting food and urine and
unwashed bodies. We try to get comfortable in the uncomfortable
chairs. The room is littered with candy wrappers, and the floor
is sticky. There are a few other people sitting near us who look
scared and depressed. I pick up a magazine but the words blur
too much to read it. To our left, a man lies stretched across three
chairs with his hoodie pulled over his face, snoring lightly. He
looks like he's been here for hours.

Liz checks with the desk several times to see how things are going. "Not yet," the woman says. "They'll call you."

No matter the stress level of most situations, if I'm able to exert some sort of control, I'm usually fine. But if I am helpless, I panic. I don't want to panic now. I don't want anyone to see how scared I am. I want to keep calm, at least on the outside. Corralled out in the waiting room I begin to feel like I'm abandoning Bill, but I don't seem to have a choice without causing a big ruckus. So Liz and I sit, pretending to read, make some calls, whisper to each other about how dirty the place is.

Finally, a doctor comes into the waiting room and says they are transferring Bill to the intensive care unit. He says there is serious bleeding on the brain but they have a great neurology team. They lead us to Bill's room and the smell changes to antiseptic. Liz doesn't have the bag of clothes anymore. They must be in the car. And then I realize Bill won't need his clothes for a while. We follow his gurney toward his new room, but the powers that be stop us before we go in.

They tell us to make ourselves comfortable in a different waiting room while they get him ready. This time it's a lovely clean room with real flowers here and there, tables and chairs, television, and a stunning view of the river. I think I smell coffee, but I'd be up all night if I had coffee now.

"This sure is a switch from the emergency waiting room," I say to Liz.

I wonder what they mean when they say we'll have to wait because they're "getting him ready." Ready for what? Ready to die? Ready for visitors? Ready for brain surgery?

When we're allowed into his windowless room, he's hooked up to what must be ten different machines. Each has lights blinking various colors and numbers, and each one makes a slightly different beep. But, in a way, the cramped windowless room seems deathly quiet. I take his hand and squeeze it.

"Hi, honey, you're in the hospital."
He squeezes back and looks at me with his good eye.
"You had a bad accident."
Nothing.
"The horses are fine."
He squeezes again.

From then on, the evening blurs. A brain surgeon talks about surgery to relieve the pressure, but there is too much blood to operate, and both between his brain and his skull and all throughout his brain. Another surgeon comes in and tells us that he should be in the ICU for a few days and then he will be going to rehab. Nothing seems to make sense. I feel a bit like Alice in Wonderland, eating the cake that makes you tall and then shrinking by drinking from the bottle.

I look at the man in the bed, hooked up to everything, and wonder why he would go to rehab. Rehab for what? Breathing? I don't understand any of it. I can't for the life of me envision Bill on a treadmill right now. Just this morning he was an eighty-two-year-old man who did pushups every morning, cut trees with his chainsaw, shoveled manure without even getting winded. But now he just lies in the hospital bed, unable to speak. How do they rehabilitate someone who can't even smile?

I ask questions, pretend I am totally in charge of everything. I sense that if I have even a small moment of weakness, I'll break down. The doctors tell us that there's a hotel attached to the hospital so Liz decides to check in to a room there, while I'll stay in the ICU to be close to Bill. The only chair in the room is an ugly orange straight-back plastic thing with wooden arms, but I pull it close to the bed and try to settle in for the night. I swallow a couple of prednisones so I'll be able to walk tomorrow and I make a pillow out of my old sweater. I look at Bill for a long moment, unmoving in the nest of tubes and wires, and make the "I love you" sign under my sweater so no one else sees. Then I close my eyes for what I know will be a long sleepless night.

A tall "Nurse Ratched" woman with a medical face mask is assigned to him. She's efficient, cold. I'm rather glad she's wearing a face mask because I imagine her expression to be austere and I'm not sure I want to see it. She glares at me as if I were in the way. I probably am but I don't move. She barely speaks to me except to answer questions in a brusque tone, so I stay quiet and try to sleep. That's impossible. I can't get comfortable in the chair and the plastic sticks to my skin and my clothes, so I watch him do nothing. The machines flash, and the nurse comes in and out of the room.

I watch her because I can't sleep and there's not much else to do. Although she is still brusque, I see her concern. She cares about him. I can tell. She wants to do her best and doesn't want any interference. When she moves him or cleans him, she's gentle and careful. I slowly begin to trust her. Every few minutes, I check all the machines and watch to make sure he's breathing. Then I realize there would be a warning beep to signal he hasn't taken a breath in a while. I wish they could take out the breathing tube because he might want to speak, to say that he fell against a tree or a moose spooked the horses and they ran, throwing him against a rock. He certainly couldn't talk with that tube down his throat but he doesn't even try. When I see he is awake, I speak to him, tell him again he's in the hospital, squeeze his hand, but that's all we can do for right now.

"How do you think he's doing?" I ask the next time Nurse Ratched comes in the room.

"You'll have to ask the doctor in the morning," she says.

"When do you think they'll take the breathing tube out?"

"He's not ready for that yet," she says. When she looks at me, I see her eyes have become kinder, but she's not going to tell me much. "He's comfortable right now."

I press the little light button on my watch much too often. The night passes in ten minute increments. The nurse comes in. The nurse goes out. I try to focus on things that are happening at home, like the sheep shearing that's scheduled for a couple of days from now and the first rehearsal of *Lost in Yonkers*. And who's taking care of our very naughty dog Kelpie? She is essentially Bill's dog. She follows every move he makes with her eyes. When he sits in his chair in the kitchen, Kelpie trots over and places her head on his foot. She'll be wondering where he is and why someone else is feeding her.

The morning is going to bring people. Our children. Liz from the hotel room. Shepsi from the farm. He's bringing my old flip phone and phone number list along with my prednisone and iPad so I can contact people to tell them what's happened. But what has happened? I don't even know.

I look at my watch again. It's four in the morning. The night is almost over. I try to get some sleep, adjust my position, tuck my legs under me. Each time I move to try to get comfortable, a terrible squeak comes from the plastic chair. When I wake up, it's four-thirty. Wow. A whole half-hour of sleep, but it's better than nothing. Nurse R. comes in. "You had a snooze," she says. "Bill's been awake. I think he was looking for you."

I almost kiss her. Well, not really. But I have newfound respect and affection for the very tall mean-looking masked caregiver. She gives a shit about Bill and about me.

"Bill, I'm right here. You had an accident. You're in the hospital."

Then I realize that I'm starving and thirsty. My last meal was the chicken wings at lunch yesterday and I'm not sure I've even had a glass of water. Yesterday lunchtime seems days away. I go over the timeline of events and they all blend together in one big nightmarish movie.

Chapter 8

ᎢAMING ᎢHE ᏞAND

The old abandoned farmhouse and grown-over land we called home when we first arrived needed tons of work to turn it into a farm. The house hadn't been lived in full time since the 1940s, but had been used as a "couple of weeks every summer" place. We had worked hard and saved as much as we could before we came to Maine to make sure we would have enough money to do what we needed to do and to tide us over until we could start to bring in some income and, fortunately, the restoration of our 1715 Cape Cod house turned a good profit.

The sheep we brought with us from Massachusetts needed some page-wire fencing to keep them from leaving the farm. The whole place had only a couple of small cleared areas the size of our kitchen, and one was next to the barn. We dug about eight postholes by hand, sunk some cedar posts that Bill cut down, and strung the wire fencing on them for the sheep.

Besides Amy's pony Willow, we'd brought our Quarter Horse named Fred up from Massachusetts. We fenced off a few spots we didn't want them to walk on, but otherwise they had the run of the place. They trotted down the woodsy lane to the ocean, chewed on brush here and there, and, fortunately, avoided going down the driveway to the road.

That spring, we cleared a small plot behind the house for our first Maine garden. That year was mostly spent pulling witch grass from the rows of carrots and peas and potatoes and putting up more fencing so the horses wouldn't eat everything we had planted. The few carrots that grew were about the size of my little finger. We planted more seed potatoes than we harvested at the end of the season. But it was a start. Bill tilled the ground with the ponies and we worked the tilled soil with our hands until it was as free of rocks as we could get it. I could see the difference, and the smell of the weeds and earth was intoxicating. We added compost, lime, and rock phosphate to the soil, which was very acidic and dead, and hoped for a better garden the next season.

After a year or two the difference in the gardens was astounding. Dandelions grew because the lime made the soil more alkaline. Worms invaded the garden and where we couldn't find one worm to go fishing when we first arrived, now we had a worm farm. And finally we were getting control of the damn witch grass, which sent its tentacles out in all directions.

We were ecstatic with our choice to move to this rugged and rocky old farm on the edge of tidal West Bay near Schoodic Point, which is a branch of Acadia National Park. It was as if we were born to do this and had been just waiting for an opportunity.

Bill and I were very different in our approach to work. He worked slowly and methodically—he called it "pickin' away at it." But he got things done. He built a workshop using an attachment to his chainsaw to cut logs, which had been harvested from our woodlot, into usable beams. The device was a small metal guide that bolted to the blade of a chainsaw, enabling it to cut two by fours and planks, but the work was laborious.

Bill cleared acres of land almost singlehandedly, with some help from our Alpine goats and enthusiastic apprentices. And he tilled up new garden spots with Willow paired with two other ponies the same size that we bought from an old farmer named George, who was downsizing. A born Mainer who lived a few miles away, George had lots of advice, most of it good, but some not so good. He was very knowledgeable but not kind to his animals. However, Bill gained confidence and learned how to train horses from him. Every day, Bill hitched them up using harnesses he gleaned from farmers' junk piles, altering them to fit the small ponies.

In contrast, I worked fast and not always carefully. I got things done, too, just in a different way. The addition to the kitchen was mostly my project after Bill constructed the beams, studs, and walls. I laid the slate floor and made the work island, drawers, cabinets, and shelves.

We gathered apples in the fall up and down the road to make cider and jelly and applesauce for the winter. We bought an antique cider press with some friends and kept it for all to use. Pressed and frozen or canned, the cider kept us going all winter. We found an old abandoned farm where raspberries hung heavy on their vines and we could pick gallons in no time to make jams and jellies. Raspberry is absolutely king of the jelly world and I made enough for us and to give away.

There was no such thing as a day off, but we often had clam-bakes down at the granite shore using a small wagon Bill built for the ponies to haul pots for steaming clams, salads, vegetables, and pies down to the fire pit. The clams we dug during low tide and stored in the cool shade until we were ready to light the fire.

The next two years saw great improvement in the gardens. Our carrots finally amounted to something; the second year we packed some in peat moss down in our cool root cellar, keeping them fresh and crisp until spring. Our root cellar overflowed with carrots, beets, potatoes, leeks, tomato sauce, pickles, ketchup, jams, and jellies. The leeks we stood in pans of sand and the potatoes we stored between grain bags. Shelves already covered the walls of the cellar and we filled them with bread-and-butter pickles, kosher dills, pickled beets, and lots of other preserves.

Bags of onions hung from nails in the wall of our spare room upstairs and the bureau was full of squash, and as a result it was dubbed the "bureau of squash." We grew several sizes of pumpkins, as well as squash, including delicata (my favorite), buttercup, and red kuri (Bill's favorite). Our freezer was packed with peas and beans, frozen right out of the garden, broccoli, cauliflower, spinach—whatever wouldn't last in the root cellar or upstairs in the spare room.

We built a primitive farm stand next to the farmhouse and finally began to sell some vegetables and yarn, but we were a long way from supporting ourselves from the farm. We were beginning to see the possibilities, however. We sold a few lambs for meat and breeding stock, and I sold quite a bit of yarn that I spun from our wool.

And the best part of everything is that we both loved our new life of hard work, taking care of animals, milking, gardening, and putting food by.

Chapter 9

THE FIRST DAY IN ICU

Liz rushes into the hospital room very early in the morning. "How is he? How was your night?"

It was terrible, in truth, but I answer, "It was OK. He's about the same. Mostly sleeping. They have him pretty well sedated."

"You won't believe the tunnel to the hotel," Liz says. "It's miles long and I think it's haunted. There are weird doors, some open, some closed, old furniture stacked on other old furniture, and sharp turns back and forth."

I think she must be exaggerating but I don't tell her that. I think this is the first night she's ever spent away from her children, Harbor and Cedar, who just turned seven and four. She's clearly a wreck but she's so kind. I wish I could assuage her fears, but I feel we're in for a long haul and hope we can all keep it together for as long as we need to.

Our daughters, Sara and Amy, are on their way from Portland, which is about three hours away from Bangor. Our son, Tom, and his girlfriend, Riley, are coming. In addition to my iPad, flip phone, and phone number list from the kitchen wall, Shepsi is bringing some real food from the farm. I've been so spoiled by eating our farm food for years that it's hard to live on junk from a machine or even meals made in the cafeteria.

Liz and I talk in low voices about how Bill is doing and what we think might have happened. One thing we do know is that he wasn't kicked in the head by a horse. It's still the rumor around the hospital.

"Oh, I heard his horse kicked him."

"Hi, Bill, did you get kicked in the head?"

"Do you remember getting kicked?"

Doctors, nurses, pulmonary specialists, everyone says something like it. I tell them that isn't possible. His head would have gashes from the caulks on their shoes. But the myth persists.

Liz will go home today with my car to take care of everything there. Animals and seedlings won't survive if the farmers just leave. So someone has to be there. I'll move to the hotel. I can't imagine going home an hour and a half away and leaving Bill here.

I get messages from our granddaughters, Leila and Brianna, who are attending an indigenous peoples' gathering in New Zealand with their mother, Sheila, and stepdad, Seppy. They'll be here as soon as they can.

I stay seated in the ugly plastic chair, keeping my hand near his. When I squeeze his hand, he finally squeezes back but it's so hesitant I get the feeling that it's an effort and he isn't sure he's doing it quite right. The air is heavy in this room with no windows. It's dark and silent except for the beeping of the machines and the soft whooshes of nurses and attendants coming and going. The room smells of bleach.

Bill's big eye is still enormous, still covered by his eyelid, although it might have diminished a bit overnight. I constantly swallow my fear. There's no time for that. I'm his ear and mouthpiece. I need to keep it together.

A team comes in to take him for another CT scan, so I'm alone in the room. Someone says they will come and get me when he gets back. Liz has gone home. Sara and Amy haven't arrived yet. I go out to the waiting room, gulp a glass of water, sit in a comfortable chair, and yearn, for a moment, to be in the river that flows right by. I'm glad I'm alone in the waiting room. I don't want anyone to really think I'd jump in the river.

A loud family comes in with take-out food in Styrofoam containers and monopolize the room. It isn't even ten o'clock. Suddenly I'm hungry for something. Fresh eggs or a piece of fruit. The strong smell of soy sauce is everywhere as they open their containers and divvy up the food. I move to be closer to the door into the unit. They turn up the TV and comment on everything in loud voices that seem out of place. They don't talk about who they might know in ICU, or what their medical problem might be. I stay as long as I can stand it and make my way back to Bill's room where I sit alone, in the plastic chair, in the windowless room with the empty bed, and wait.

I snooze a bit, since I hardly slept at all during the night, until people begin to arrive. Tom and Riley come in, asking questions I can't answer."What happened? Did he get kicked?"

"Did he fall off the wagon?"

"What do they say? Is he going to be OK?" We wait in silence for them to bring him back from the scan. Only two people are allowed in the ICU rooms, but Nurse Ratched has been replaced by a male nurse who doesn't seem to care.

Finally, they wheel Bill back into the room and turn him so he's more comfortable. "What does the scan show?" I ask.

"The surgeon will be in shortly," one of the attendants says.

The waiting seems endless. Bill is awake but when I ask him what happened in those woods, he stares back with his little eye as if to say, "What woods?"

Amy and Sara finally arrive, grief stricken. Bill's eye twinkles when he sees who is hugging him and saying, "Dad, Dad." Sara has worked for a doctor for years and knows just what to say and who to ask. We take turns going to the waiting room to make calls or grab something to eat, but I'm worried about leaving him, thinking that I'll never see him again. Then I realize that's true no matter what happens. At one moment, I believe he's gone and this is some other person in his body. At the next, I see a flicker in his eye and believe he's in there, scrambling to get out.

Finally one of the surgeons comes into the room and I am in his face. "What does the CT show? Is he still bleeding? Are you going to operate?"

I know I'm obnoxious but I don't give a fuck. Let them think I'm a lunatic. Then I realize that I'm appearing perfectly normal to them and they are kind. They ask questions.

"Was he a social being?"

"He was quiet, didn't say a lot, but he loved working at the town office and socializing with friends."

"Did he get any exercise?"

"Exercise? You've never met anyone, especially his age, who gets so much exercise."

"Did he drink or use drugs?"

"I've never seen him inebriated in forty-five years. But, yes, he loved a good martini and had a beer if it was a hot day."

Finally, I say, "Look, let me tell you about this man. He got up every day at four-twenty and did his pushups. He shoveled manure, cut wood with his chainsaw. He was a town selectman. He hauled logs from the woods with a team of horses named Andy and Star, horses he trained to do what he said and to pull hard. He played bop jazz on his drum kit as loud and as musical as anyone. We had 'old people sex' if we felt up to it. And after dinner, he sometimes had a martini in his chair. Once over forty-five years ago, he smoked a joint laced with something scary that wasn't pot and he never smoked another one."

"Let's look at the CT," the doctor with a Caribbean accent, Dr. Grant, says as he flips on the screen and points to spots here and there, between Bill's brain and skull and rivers of blood throughout the brain. "There doesn't seem to be any new bleeding but there's a lot of blood already there."

"Do you operate to lessen it?"

"We'll have to wait for it to be absorbed. It could be a few days before we take him up to rehab."

Rehab? Rehab again? They work with him on his walking and talking? Talking? The only things he's said since the accident are "horses" and "off." He hasn't tried to talk at all. Even with that tube down his throat, shouldn't he try to talk? Or at least move his mouth?

Shepsi comes in, looking ashen. He has food for me from the farm. Carrots, coleslaw, real food that I can eat. He also has my iPad, phone, and phone list. I grab the iPad. Shepsi looks out of place here, just like Bill does. His blond dreadlocks hang down past his waist and he's wearing clean farm clothes. His hands show that he's been working hard.

"Look," I say, turning on the iPad and bringing up a great photo of Bill driving the horses in the red logging arch. "Here he is. This is what he was. This is the vehicle he was driving when the accident happened." I look over at Bill and he doesn't react at all. "He wraps a chain around the log and the other end wraps around the back of the logging arch. When he gives the word, the horses step up and drag the log to wherever he wants to leave it."

"Are those the horses that kicked him in the head?" one of the surgeons asks.

My voice rises. "No horse kicked him. No. No. We don't know what happened. Or where it happened."

Suddenly I feel that if I knew what happened and where it happened, I could make things better. The room is packed with people. They are all looking at me to see what I'm going to say next. I don't want them to think that Bill used to look like he does now, with his protruding eye lid, tubes coming out of his mouth, heart monitors stuck all over his bare chest.

His glasses. Where are they? He always wears his glasses, especially if he's working. There were no glasses in the road where Aaron found him. No one said they found glasses. They weren't with his clothes.

"His glasses," I say. I know it's too loud. "Where are they? Where are they?" I look from one person to another. "We need to find his glasses. They must be in the woods. No one found them in the road. And they weren't in the bag of clothes at the hospital. Where are they?"

I look around the room.

"Where are his glasses?"

I bite my lip, waiting for some kind of response but there is none. The room is deathly quiet. I feel like jelly inside. They don't understand what I'm trying to say. They all stare back at me as if to say, "He doesn't need his glasses now."

I say, "We will know what happened to Bill when we find his glasses."

Chapter 10

APPRENTICE STORIES

Over the years we've farmed this land, we have mentored well over two hundred apprentices, most coming here through MOFGA. But some found us because they were our students back in Massachusetts, and a few were relatives or friends of relatives.

They arrived by thumb or bus or their own car or were driven by a friend or parent, carrying backpacks and suitcases full of old clothes, books about farming, banjoes and fiddles, a secret stash of weed. Some were fantastic workers and great friends. Some were nightmares. And it seemed impossible to tell from an interview or a phone conversation whether they would work out or not.

Early on we had apprentices like Jeff and Will and Ann and Harry and Sheila and Peg and Keith and Annie and Bob who worked hard, wanted to learn as much as they could, and loved what they were doing. In the early days, we all lived right in the farmhouse together with our kids. Before we had apprentice housing, we shared cleaning and cooking, went to the shore together for clambakes, spun and knit in the evenings, and became fast friends. Cleaning day was always Saturday afternoon to the tunes of Frank Zappa. My cousin was a member of the Mothers of Invention, Frank Zappa's band in the 1960s, and I introduced Bill to Zappa—the man and his music. Bill loved the crazy lyrics Frank wrote and appreciated his genius. It was ideal background music for house cleaning.

We built apprentice housing when it became too crowded in the farmhouse and we felt that we and the apprentices needed some space. Our next-door neighbors were trying to get rid of an A-frame cottage, so we hired a truck and trailer to haul it up the driveway. We set it down on cement blocks. That would house one or two apprentices. And the wood for the new two-bedroom apprentice house on the path down to the shore, which would house two more, was all cut with the new sawmill.

And they kept coming. From Ecuador, Denmark, California, Florida, New Jersey, Florida, Scotland. They were all in search of "The Good Life" à la Scott and Helen Nearing, early advocates of simple living, whom we knew well in those days. Most apprentices were incredible people who enabled us to branch out, grow for the market, and become a commercial enterprise.

Romances kept switching back and forth, making for loads of speculation and gossip. A few weddings even came out of apprentice adventures. And, needless to say, there was a number of breakups of couples who came together and fell apart under the stress of farm life. Because we lived and worked so closely on the farm, bickering and fighting was plain to everyone. It made us all uncomfortable if a couple wasn't getting along and horrified if we suspected any physical abuse, which did happen once.

My cousin's friend's daughter from California wanted a farm apprentice experience so we told her to come. She arrived ready to work, and she did. But all her clothes were white and therefore got pretty dirty doing farm work. She changed several times a day, into new white work clothes, which necessitated many loads of laundry. That was fine if we had sunny weather but if it rained, it was a problem because we had no dryer.

There was the fellow from New York who did massage work and ended up having an affair with our neighbor's wife, which didn't sit well with the neighbor. And then there was Alex, the fellow from Scotland who had a pet cockroach back home. Bill took Alex to the immigration office in Bangor to prove he had enough money to support himself. Bill handed him a thousand dollars on the way to the meeting, which he handed back on the ride home. The man in the office said Alex couldn't do any work at all, even dishes, without breaking the immigration laws so he'd certainly better not be out in the field. One very rainy day, the man drove up in a government vehicle, pounded on the door, and asked for Alex.

"He's upstairs," Bill said.

The man went up and found Alex writing a letter home. I can't help but think he chose a rainy day so Alex wouldn't be working in violation of the law. Alex ended up making puffin pull toys to sell to make money to ride his bicycle all the way to Mexico.

And there was Vivaldi, so called because he was an accomplished violinist from New York who looked like a Greek god and knew it. He came to the Common Ground Fair with us that September. There he helped shovel trenches to keep the Wednesday Spinners' tent from flooding, all done shirtless. It was hard to keep from staring because it was, indeed, a beautiful sight.

We had two apprentices who were terrific until they had psychotic breaks in the middle of the workday and left in the throes of mania. They were some of the best workers we had and we loved having them. One of them, a gorgeous dancer and sweet soul, just cracked in the middle of the afternoon and caught the next bus home. I've seen her since and she's dancing again.

Parents and lovers came to visit, which added to the gossip factory, and many became good friends. Brothers Jeff and Tom tried to outdo each other cooking. I taught them to spin wool and knit socks, but their socks were so stiff they could have been lethal weapons. But we loved them. We lost something when all the apprentices moved to the apprentice house or the A-frame.

Some events over the years were difficult at the time but have now become humorous. A teenager named Hugh came from Rhode Island for the summer and he had shingled most of one side of the barn at a huge slant before we realized he was quite autistic and wasn't fond of straight lines. My seven-year-old nephew, Josh, was here for the summer at the time and became great friends with Hugh. Once, Hugh spent the whole day cooking for Bill and me, a couple of other apprentices, and Josh, using food that we had grown in the garden. We all sat down and Hugh proudly served his dinner, waiting for comments with great anticipation. It was a casserole of some kind and had a very bitter taste but we ate small bites while praising his cooking.

Finally, Josh said. "This is the worst meal I have ever had. I'm not eating any more." And he put down his fork. That opened the conversation.

"Hugh," I said. "What did you put in the dinner? Show me where you got it."

Hugh took me out to the herb garden and pointed to my patch of wormwood that I grew to use in warding off moths in the wool and fleas on the animals. We called poison control for information. The woman on the phone said that thujone, which is found in wormwood, can cause seizures, nightmares, vomiting, paralysis, and death. That was the end of Hugh's dinner. We were told to watch for symptoms and to call back if any became evident. I guess we hadn't eaten enough to kill us, but poor Hugh was devastated that his first and only cooking experience ended in disaster.

Another time, Kelpie became sluggish and wouldn't get off the porch. Finally I dragged her to the lawn where she immediately fell over. I set her upright and she fell over again.

"Bill," I said. "There's something very wrong with Kelpie." She was lying on her side and not responding at all. "I think she's dying. You've got to get her to the vet. I'll call ahead."

Bill carried her to the truck and drove out of the yard faster than usual. I called Dr. Barb to alert her that Bill was coming. I asked around to see if anyone had noticed the problem earlier. Nothing.

"Did she get into something she shouldn't have?"

No answer.

Bill came back about forty-five minutes later with bad news. Dr. Barb thought it was a neurological problem and was sending Kelpie to a canine neurologist the other side of Portland, about four and a half hours away. God knows what the vet was going to cost, let alone the travel and an overnight stay.

"I'll pack," I said. "I'll take her. Probably need to spend the night." By that time all the apprentices had gathered around to see what was going on with Kelpie. "Think, everyone. Do you know of anything bad she could have eaten?"

There was a long pause. In the meantime, Bill's friend, the chief of police, happened by, and Bill invited him into the kitchen. Just then, one of our favorite apprentices, Julien, came in.

"I think I know what happened," he said. I could tell from the look on his face that he knew something that was difficult to tell. "Kelpie ate my stash. I left it on top of the wood pile and she got into it."

"Pot? She ate your pot?"

"The whole bag."

The police chief said, "I didn't hear a thing," and put his hands over his ears. This all happened, of course, when possession of marijuana was a criminal offense.

Bill called the vet and she said that would explain it. "She'll have to sleep it off," she said. "It could take twenty-four hours. Marijuana can kill dogs if they eat it. Let's hope she's OK tomorrow." And she was, but it took almost two days of sleeping it off in her hut. The next day, Julien brought us a cake and an apology. We laugh about it now, but at the time we thought we were going to have a dead dog on our hands.

Erica and Simon, rather than being apprentices, did an exchange of work for room and board. They asked if they could bring a cat and our first inclination was a firm no, but they persisted and we needed the help so finally we said OK. It wasn't long before, instead of one cat, there were six kittens and one cat. They couldn't find homes for the little ones so those little ones grew into big ones and then we had seven cats shitting and pissing all over the sweet little A-frame cottage and by the time we asked them to leave, the place was a stinking mess and poor Liz had to scour the whole place.

Nathan found us by accident, seemed like a lost soul, but we thought he'd be a good help. He very quickly hooked up with our female apprentice from New York and, since she had a car and he didn't, she made the mistake of loaning him her grandmother's pristine vintage sedan. I happened to be still up the night he had taken the car to go to a MOFGA meeting when the phone rang. It was Nathan.

"You need to come and get me," he said. "I had an accident and I'm at the police station." It was at least three hours away and I wasn't willing to go and get him, especially in the dark. "The car is totaled."

"What the hell happened?" I said.

"I ran a red light and T-boned another car," he said. After I told him that there was no way I was going out in the dark to get him and Bill had been in bed for hours, I hung up. He called again. "I need a ride."

"Hitch," I said again before I hung up.

The next day his girlfriend drove one of our vehicles to pick him up.

A few weeks before that, Nathan had gone for a late afternoon walk across the street in the woodlot, and an apprentice sharing his cabin came over around eight to say that he hadn't come back yet and it was dark and getting late. We were ready for bed but we all went out looking for him with flashlights. Finally we called the police who brought in a tracking dog and more police. They finally found him settled down in a cabin deep in the woods in the middle of the night. He said that he was planning to spend the night there because he didn't want to bother anyone.

One night Bill and I were in my office, watching something on Netflix. We ended up taking our clothes off and having sex right on the couch. And we heard scratching at the door that goes into the greenhouse from my office and it was Nathan, asking in a quiet voice if he could borrow something. He started trying to open the door but fortunately there was a curtain across it that made it difficult to move the door very quickly. I shouted anxiously, "Now isn't a good time. Go away." I'm not sure he had any clue what an amorous adventure he had interrupted.

The stories could go on and on. Some sad. Some hilarious. A few tragic. All memorable. But of the hundreds of young people who've made their way through Darthia Farm, most have become amazing farmers, parents, and activists. We are very proud to have played even a small part in that development.

Chapter 11

THE MAGIC TUNNEL

That night, when everything becomes deathly quiet except for the beeping machines, I tell Bill again that he's had an accident and is in the hospital and that I love him. He looks at me and shrugs his arms and shoulders. I don't think he has any idea what happened. I kiss his forehead and gather up the food that people have brought from the farm, including a bottle of merlot. Everyone has gone home except for dear Sara, who is going to stay with me in the hotel. We make our way to the tunnel that will lead us from the ICU to our room. We stop at the entrance and look down the corridor.

"What is this place?" Sara says.

"Kind of creepy, isn't it."

"Oh my God. It's weirding me out."

The passageway is even stranger than Liz reported. The hospital section ends abruptly as the floor changes from green carpeting to gray cement turning into an underground tunnel right out of a horror movie. I love it, but I think Sara is terrified. It winds around and around in the dimness and the only sounds are our footsteps. There is no one else in sight and I wonder if we are in the right place until I remember Liz's comments.

We pass piled-up, broken chairs in the hallway, empty rooms with no apparent purpose, doors painted in bright colors that appear to go nowhere. The passageway turns corners and goes up and down little hills. Sara's face is ashen. I see that she expects someone to jump out at us any minute. It reminds me of Alice's rabbit hole without the Tweedledee and Tweedledum but I expect to have them jump out from one of the empty rooms any minute. Abruptly, after seemingly miles of walking through the obviously haunted underground alley, the concrete floor changes to shabby carpeting where two candy vending machines greet us on the left, as if anyone who was brave enough to go through the passage deserves and needs candy right away. We have reached the hotel.

I check the key that Liz gave me. On the right is the elevator and I press the buttons for the fourth floor. The room is sweet. Two double beds, a small dining area with two chairs and a small table, and a bathroom. I have no idea what is out the window because it's pitch dark.

I throw my few things onto the bed. Sara has the bag of food people brought to the hospital for me. I've made it through the first day of this hell. The first thing Sara does is open the wine and pours each of us each a paper cup. I hold mine up to Sara.

"To Farmer Bill," I say. And we weep into our cups.

We dig through the food. Carrots brought by Shepsi from our root cellar are the best.

Then guacamole in a bag. Some corn chips. Nice cheddar cheese. Gluten-free crackers. Olives. We spread it out on the table and it looks like we're having someone in for drinks and hors d'oeuvres. I make some calls. One to my sister in Nova Scotia. We finish off the bottle and snack a little before falling into bed.

The next morning, the vigil begins again. I, used to being very busy and productive, now sit at Bill's bedside waiting for word on test results, opinions from the surgeons, thoughts from the respiratory team about when the breathing tube will come out. When no one else is in the room, I watch the numbers on the machines blink and change.

Shepsi brings my knitting and the manuscript I was editing. If I'm going to be here for a while, I will want something to do. As it turns out, I neither knit nor edit. My concentration is shot. All I can do is watch flashing lights and sit by Bill's bed. Family and friends file in and out, people call and send emails asking how he is. I respond that he is holding his own.

Someone sets up a schedule for people to come in and sit with him so I can get a break, but I find it almost impossible to leave his side except at night when I know that I need the sleep and that he will be somewhat sedated and that I am only minutes away if I run through the tunnel. Ex-apprentices come in, some holding back tears and some not, take his hand, talk to him, tell him of any news they might have. My fellow Wednesday Spinners gather and decide who will come when to make sure someone is here with Bill and me every day. My dear friend Becky takes movies around town with her phone to show him.

"Here's the town hall and now I'm going into the Pickled Wrinkle for a beer."

"And now I'm in the town office. Everyone misses you."

"And here I am at the farm. See the sheep? And Andy and Star?"

"And here I am going into the library."

For the next few days, friends bring food, a gift box arrives from the Women's Club in town, a fruit basket arrives at home from my dear cousin Virginia in New York, and someone brings in some yummy organic pears from that basket for me. One day blends into the next. Each day I make the long haul from my hotel room to the hospital room, pull the rolling suitcase that Shepsi brought, full of food, knitting, the manuscript that I'm not working on, the schedule of visitors, my iPad. I always arrive by six in the morning and ask about his night. Sometimes Sara is with me. Sometimes my nurse practitioner friend and fellow spinner, Wendy. Sometimes Becky. Sometimes Amy. And sometimes I'm alone.

I'm not afraid of the mystery doors and dark passageways, or perhaps I really am afraid but I love being scared. Fear invigorates me. When I'm walking through the tunnel alone, I pretend I'm in some kind of magical place that will transform everything and when I come out the other end he'll be standing there at the hospital entrance wearing his jeans, hefting his chainsaw. But when I arrive at his room, the illusion bursts, and there he is in his johnny, lying in the windowless room hooked up to a tangle of wires.

They try to remove the breathing tube, but he isn't ready. I feel some guilt because I wanted it removed. I wanted him to tell us what happened and try to smile. He has no gag reflex yet and develops pneumonia. But still the doctors talk about rehab.

Dr. Grant, the sweet man from St. Kitts who seems genuinely interested in who Bill was and is, orders a room with a view. He says that no farmer who works outside all day should be in a room without windows. My granddaughters, Leila and Brianna, return from New Zealand with Sheila and Seppy. They give me a sacred necklace from the Maori, a beautiful green teardrop stone that I wear every day. I can feel its heat and power on my bare chest when I have it on. And still we wait. Wait for a room with a view, wait for the blood to be absorbed into his brain, wait until we can safely try removing the breathing tube again.

Back home on the farm, Donna comes to shear the sheep, and lambing begins. Pam and Susanne, two of the spinners, are helping. Susanne sends me an email to fill me in.

"We had the most pleasant shearing I've ever been to. More helpers than sheep. Very quiet, peaceful and quick. Fleeces were very good. Several were spectacular. One had dandruff, though. Identity cards are in each bag with the name. We swept out the

dye shed and fleeces are loosely tied up in bags on the back shelf."
My dye shed is right next to the barn and that's where I do all my
fleece washing and plant dyeing in the warmer months. "Today
was extremely therapeutic for all of us. We long to be around you
guys doing something useful."

I get more email reports about the quality of the wool, the
number of lambs born, and how *Lost in Yonkers,* the play just
beginning production the day of the accident, is faring; it is being
directed by the ensemble until I return to get the play on its feet.

Day after day I walk back and forth through the magic
tunnel, hauling my rolling suitcase full of food, wine, and work.
At night I have a glass of red and dates that my friend Colleen
brought, or beef jerky from one of the spinners, or yogurt from
my friend who has a goat farm. I don't go outside at all. I still
have no idea what's outside my hotel window because I've never
been here during the daylight hours.

I'm terrified to leave him except to go to the hotel where I
know they can reach me and I can be with him in minutes. Cards
come to his room and I read them. He responds to questions with
nods and raised eyebrows, and by squeezing my hand. He looks
at me when I call his name, and every day he shrugs at least once,
a question as physical gesture. There are other good signs. When
our friend Carol comes in with a card, he takes it in his hands and
looks at it as if he's reading it. He opens it and turns it to see the
back. I know he's reading it. I think it's a big step forward and I
send out my bulletin to Facebook and the email list.

"Bill had a good day today. He read Carol's card with
curiosity, turned it back and forth, opened it and seemed happy.
Brianna, our granddaughter, came to visit today. Sinai, Maiah,
and Ella, our adoptive grandchildren whom he dearly loves,
came in to see him, bringing cheese and yogurt for me. Bill had
a session with speech therapy, which didn't go terribly well, but
he watched some hockey on the television. Tom and Riley came

to visit. They've ordered new glasses because his were lost in the accident. They are ready. So now Bill will have glasses."

He seems better and better but the doctors say he still has a lot of blood in and around his brain that needs to be absorbed. More and more waiting. Dr. Grant asks Bill again and again, "Thumbs up?" but Bill shrugs and looks at me. For guidance? For the answer? I don't know.

His room always has too many people in it. I tell everyone to please not make a lot of noise. The doctors want him quiet. Sometimes a nurse tells us to leave, but I never leave unless it's for a few minutes to get a coffee. Nurse Ratched is the worst but the best. She doesn't tolerate more than two people in his room, but I know she's a very good nurse and cares about Bill. I'm still not sure what she looks like because I haven't seen her without her surgical mask, probably to protect her from the flu, which is working its way through the hospital.

Our friends and family are amazingly kind and helpful. I've been running down to the gift shop to get the newspaper every day because we always read the newspaper together. Susan, one of the spinners, buys a subscription for me and now it gets delivered to the hospital room early in the morning. For a moment it takes my mind off the machines and Bill's restlessness.

We'd been in the ICU almost two weeks when things begin to happen. Dr. Grant comes in again and says, "Bill, we're moving you to a room with a view."

Bill looks at me. He knows.

Dr. Grant comes back in the afternoon to check on him. "Bill, we're still trying to get you a room with a window. You'd like that."

Bill looks over at him and shrugs but the shrug seems to be his answer to everything.

"Bill, can you give me a thumbs up?" Dr. Grant says.

I almost say again that I'm not sure that's in Bill's vocabulary when I see his thumbs on both hands stick straight up in the air.

"There," I say. "He did it." I have to fight to keep myself from yelling, "Hallelujah!" "He knows. He's following directions. That's great, Bill. You did it."

And I give Bill a thumbs-up. Then I realize that it isn't a contest. It's not a game. He doesn't get points if he gets it right. One small step toward rehab.

His cyclops eye opens. It's the first time I've seen that eye since the day of the accident.

It looks fine. Like the other one. Twinkly and the palest shade of blue.

When the medical people leave the room, I give him another thumbs-up and an "I Love You" sign. When they come back in, there's lots of talk about plans. They decide to perform a tracheostomy so they can remove the breathing tube. I know what that means because our daughter, Robin, had a tracheostomy for several months when she was a teenager and had jaw surgery. They have the tracheostomy planned for tomorrow. They will make a small hole just above the breastbone and through it insert a tube into his throat. The patient breathes through the tube rather than through the mouth, making inhalation and exhalation easier and more direct.

"Bill, they're going to take out that breathing tube." His eyes tell me that he understands. He hasn't smiled or attempted to speak since the accident, but his blue eyes, both wide open now, show that he knows.

The other thing they discuss is putting in a stomach tube to feed him some real food and not just liquid from the IV drip. I guess that will be better, healthier, contribute more to his healing. They cut a small hole through his abdomen into his stomach and insert a rubber tube. When he comes back from the procedure, my spinner friend, Julie, who is also a midwife visiting a patient upstairs, asks to look at the label from the food they're going to be giving him. She shows it to me.

As organic farmers for forty-five years, we know what real food is. I scan down the list of ingredients and for the life of me I can't find any word that I've ever heard before. They are all long unpronounceable chemical names that can't be good for anyone.

"You can get real organic food for stomach tubes," Julie says. "I'm going to find out."

I can tell from the look on the nurses' faces that they're not crazy about the idea but one says she'll check into it. When she comes back, she tells us that that insurance might not cover it and that it is very expensive.

I think of Robin's diet those months after her surgery. Just whatever we were having for dinner mushed up in a blender. The whole expensive food in a bag thing seems like a scam, but we ask for the organic real food. Seems kind of amusing considering his last meal before the accident was two red hot dogs but I don't mention that. When they bring the bag of food, we again read the ingredients and it is, indeed, real food. Kale, squash, spinach, potatoes, some other vegetables. No red hot dogs, alas. At least it's real food and I've heard of all of the ingredients. It's certainly worth the extra money. He hasn't eaten anything with his mouth since the accident and I am sad he can't taste any of the food even though it doesn't look terribly appetizing. They hook up the bag to the stomach tube and hang the bag on the rack with the IVs. Kind of creepy to be funneling food directly into his stomach but it's better than getting fed through his vein.

"Look, Bill," I say. "Thanksgiving dinner in a bag." I read the list of veggies to him. He looks at me and shrugs as if to say, "Where's the turkey?"

Chapter 12

ꝶHANKSGIVING

I recently came across a Thanksgiving menu from some years ago that made me remember my Keynote Address at the Common Ground Fair, in which I asked the public to try to have a meal every month that is mostly organic. Almost all our meals consisted of organic food from right on Darthia Farm. Here's our menu for a Thanksgiving meal for ten people.

> *Stuffed Clams*
> *Potato Leek Soup*
> *Cranberry Sorbet*
> *Roast Turkey*
> *Sausage Cranberry Stuffing*
> *Mashed Potatoes*
> *Brussels Sprouts*
> *Candied Carrots*
> *Creamed Onions*
> *Beet and Neuchâtel Cheese Salad*
> *Cranberry Apple Pie*
> *Blueberry Pie*

Bill dug clams for the hors d'oeuvres down the lane at the edge of the bay during low tide. I mixed chopped steamed clams

Me holding a turkey. We raised turkeys for many years. I loved them alive and I loved them on a platter.

with sautéed onions, garlic, butter, salt and pepper, a dash of paprika and chopped parsley, sprinkled it with dried breadcrumbs and baked it all in the clam shells until brown—everything gleaned from our farm except for the spices and the wheat in the breadcrumbs.

Potatoes for the soup were planted in furrows plowed by Bill and the horses. He loved potatoes so he worked hard to keep them hilled, which helped with weed control and kept the potatoes from being exposed to the sun, causing them to become green and therefore poisonous to eat. The furrows for the leeks were made in the same way as the furrows for the potatoes. We planted seedlings from our greenhouse in the furrows and as they grew, we filled in the furrows and the tiny leeks turned into fat stalks. Finally we mounded soil up around them, covering the stem of the leek and blanching it, making it white and tender.

The milk and cream used in the soup came from our big-eyed Jersey cow, Tammy Faye, who was named after the evangelical wife of Jim Bakker and who wore way too much eye makeup, which ran down her cheeks when she cried. We had a visiting niece one summer who loved to make fun of *The PTL Club* with Jim and Tammy Faye, so we watched it when we could stand it.

We had been raising turkeys for many years, almost from the beginning. Our first few years, we slaughtered sixty turkeys, which took us two days. In those early years we didn't have the shop to work in and many times it was freezing cold and snowing when we slaughtered. Now we have a good team who knows what they are doing and we do thirty to forty in a day. I'm the kitchen person who makes sure all the guts are out, cleans up the birds, does a little last-minute plucking, weighs and prices them, sucks the air out of the bags with the vacuum cleaner. Wendy's husband, Henri, along with apprentices and friends with sharp knives, slit the turkeys' throats so they bleed out. The pluckers dip the carcasses in hot water, swish them around, and plop them on the table where they pull out the feathers.

The turkeys go from the outside killing area into the workshop where Wendy and Bill gut and clean the inside of the birds, remove the feet, trim the neck and send them in to me for the finish work. Everyone who gets a turkey from us raves that it's by far the best turkey they ever ate. I'm sure it's because they run free and eat lots of bugs and grass, and they're happy birds.

The stuffing varies every year. That year, I concocted a sausage and cranberry stuffing with my sourdough bread. The sausage came from our pigs, which we slaughtered with help of an apprentice. We had the butcher shop grind the scraps and shoulders and we made many pounds of sausage. We spread out a plastic sheet over the kitchen table and dumped the meat on it. Then we added the fennel, cumin, coriander, hot pepper, salt, pepper, red wine, onions, garlic, and mixed it with our hands, being careful to not mix too much or get the meat too warm. We put the meat through the old manual meat grinder with the sausage attachment forcing it into the casings, which we made from the pigs' small intestines. Each link is tied off with cotton string and then they go into the freezer.

Cleaning the casings isn't for the faint of heart, although I enjoy it and some apprentices have added it to their skills list. The nozzle of the hose fits into one end of a small intestine, which Bill has pulled out of the carcasses. I slowly turn on the water in the hose until I see it's forcing all the excrement out onto the ground, holding the end tight against the nozzle. I carefully, with a dull dinner knife against a wooden cutting board, scrape the intestines, removing both the inside and outside layers of flesh at once until the intestine is almost transparent. Then they all go into a bowl full of cold water mixed with baking soda and salt in the refrigerator until the next day when the procedure is repeated. If they are cleaned properly, they are clear and odorless and without holes.

That year our friends brought us wild cranberries they gleaned along a river in northern Maine. We used the cranberries to make the sorbet palate cleanser, the stuffing, and the cranberry apple pie.

The vegetables were all grown here on the farm. Bill harvested the Brussels sprouts from the garden Thanksgiving Day because a few freezes sweeten the sprouts. The potatoes and carrots came from the root cellar where they had been carefully stored after the October harvest. Onions had been hanging on a nail upstairs in the guest room since mid-September. The maple syrup for the carrots was given to us by our dear friend, Becky, who lives deep in the woods in a cabin she and Art originally built for five hundred dollars. They raised their children there with no electricity or running water, and they made a damn good maple syrup.

The beet and cheese salad was made with both golden and red beets from the root cellar and creamy herbed cheese that we made from Tammy Faye's milk.

And the best for last—the pies. Cranberries from Geri and Donna, apples from all around the farm, blueberries Bill and the apprentices raked from Harry's blueberry field. The pie crust used store-bought flour but the lard to bind it together was made here on the farm with fat back and leaf fat from our pigs.

Bill and I cut the fat into egg-sized chunks and put them into a hotel pan that fits into the oven. We heated it until the fat was rendered and crispy chunks remained floating on top. Lots of people eat the cracklings but I'm not one of them. The chickens got the cracklings after the lard was strained. We stored the lard in the freezer in one-pound packages. It's the best for baking pies and cookies, and frying.

We still try to eat mostly from the farm but I did buy things like fresh mushrooms when I didn't have enough gathered from the woods. And sad to say, we didn't make the bright red hot dogs that Bill loved and was only allowed to eat very occasionally.

Chapter 13

FINDING A BOP DRUMMER

The lovely Dr. Grant expedites Bill's move to a room with a window that has a great view of the river and trees beyond. I haven't seen the outside for almost two weeks and I'm surprised to see that most of the snow has gone, leaving brown patches along the banks of rushing water. The new room has more space, which helps when I lug in the manuscript I'm not working on, my knitting, food for the day, the list of who is coming to visit. Each day when I send out a bulletin about Bill's progress, I receive hundreds of comments back from people, some of whom I don't even know. The list grows and grows until there are over a thousand followers.

From my sister: "Any new update? I hate to bug you but love you both so much!"

From my actors: "I know you're not a huggy person but tough shit—we're sending you hugs anyway."

From Sara: "Take care of him. I know you will."

From the farm: "Kelpie is doing just fine. She's getting lots of walks to the beach and through the forest."

From ex-apprentice Chris: "I just heard Bill was in a bad accident. May I come this week? Please?"

Bill drumming. He practiced to Dizzy and Monk CDs whenever he could. I never complained because I played the bagpipes.

From my friends Susan, Aran, Margot: "We are thinking about you and Bill all the time—with love."

From Bill's dear friend, Eve: "Sending a kiss on the cheek to both of you and a big hug as well."

And hundreds more.

I have said visitors are welcome but to please let me know first. Friends and neighbors from Gouldsboro come. Spinners get on the list—Judy, Susanne, Penelope—women whom I've known for over forty years and new spinners who have recently joined the group. Folks from town government arrive and fill him in about the latest workings of the town. My theater people come and my writer friend, Annaliese, drags me away for a quick lunch in the cafeteria. My first lunch away from the unit.

Bill looks at them and it seems his eyes say he knows who's sitting talking to him. The visitors give me a chance for a little break, but when I leave him I panic, so I usually just take a little walk around the unit and come right back. Sometimes I want to say, "Go away so I can have him to myself," but I don't. He needs me to be there calmly holding his hand, telling him he's had an accident and is in the hospital, not screaming swear words like a banshee.

Amy and Sara come as often as they can but it's not easy for them. Portland is three hours away and they both have jobs. Of course, there's no sign of Alison, Bill's daughter, who, for some reason no one knows, wants nothing to do with us and has barely spoken to us in almost twenty years. One of her daughters, Susie, comes in to visit with Brianna, which couldn't have been easy for her. She's a senior in high school and has hardly spoken a word to us in her whole life. It's awkward, but I say, "Bill, Susie is here to see you." He shrugs.

Sara's new boyfriend, Duane, often drives her up and does paperwork for his contracting business in the family waiting room after he sees Bill, while Sara visits. He is a treasure. He goes to a great little restaurant downtown and gets sandwiches for everyone. The town selectmen have sent a gift certificate for the restaurant, which is an amazingly perfect thing to have done. We feed the whole family out in the waiting room.

Bill is a bop jazz drummer and he has a coffeehouse gig with the Bill Thayer Porch Band coming up at the "Last Friday Coffee House," in Winter Harbor. He's been playing jazz drums since he was barely a teenager and still practices several times a week. The band got started from the Piano on the Porch Parties we've thrown every August for decades. Years ago, we used to haul our big old upright out the door and onto the porch. Usually over a hundred people parked in our mowed pasture and walked up the driveway carrying casserole dishes, salad bowls, chips and salsa, boxes of homemade chocolate chip cookies, cheesecakes, pies, wine, and beer, to listen to some great bebop and to hear our chorus sing—but mostly they came for the jazz. We always roasted a turkey, and sometimes, Donna brought clams for steaming. Over the years, the piano idea evolved into the pianist bringing a portable piano but everything else stayed the same except for musicians and party-goers cycling in and out.

Bill's been really excited about the gig because he hasn't performed in a while, so I know how important this is for him. Our friend Tom is coming up from Massachusetts to play lead trumpet and will stay at our farmhouse in Gouldsboro. We've got a couple of great sax players, a pianist, a bassist, but there's no drummer. It's been on Bill's calendar for months and he was really hyped to play again with these great musicians. We scramble; I call around. Beau Lisey is busy that night, Mike Bennett is going to be out of town, wishes he could do it. Finally, the other musicians find a woman from Blue Hill, Lynette Woods, who is free and plays bop jazz. I tell Bill. He shrugs again, but I know he's pleased. We arrange for a live feed into the hospital room so Bill can see and hear the great bunch of musicians trading fours and improvising on Dizzy Gillespie and Charlie Parker tunes.

The young woman from rehab comes in mid-morning the day before the coffeehouse gig. "Bill, how are you this morning?"

He shrugs.

"I'm from Rehab. I'd like to get you sitting up today."

Oh, my God, I think. *There really is a rehab.*

She cradles Bill in her arms and slides him into a sitting position at the edge of the bed. I study his face for some kind of expression. His face is blank, but he is sitting up. I'm amazed at the strength he still has in his upper body and neck to keep his head up. The technician continues to support him so he won't fall back. She is patient and gentle.

"Shall we try to stand up?"

She makes a small attempt to bring Bill to his feet but sees he's too weak.

"Maybe tomorrow," she says, and carefully lowers Bill back down.

I have constant flashes of us sitting on our porch months and years from now, watching Shepsi drive the wagon pulled by Star and Andy while Bill shrugs over and over and over.

Chapter 14

FARM PARTIES AND WEDDINGS

Over the years we've had many parties of all kinds because we love to share our food and we are social beings. For the first ten years or so, we had clambakes down by the ocean, inviting apprentices, ex-apprentices, family, friends from all over, visiting folks, neighbors. Our pink granite shore segues into a small sand beach to one side. In the rubble of the granite, there's a perfect spot to build a fire and cook, so Bill welded together a rack that would fit right on top of the fire pit for steaming clams and grilling meat on leftover coals. We brought everything down in the little pony cart and after doing a number of these clambakes, gathering together all the food and equipment became automatic.

We always had clams, sometimes lobsters and crabs, sometimes burgers, a big salad, potatoes wrapped in foil that we threw on the fire. One summer when my parents were visiting before my dad's Parkinson's got too bad to get down to the shore, we had one of our great clambakes. Our friends gathered, bringing casseroles, pies, all manner of yummy additions to the clam dinner. It happened to be high tide, meaning all those who wanted to could go swimming in the sun-warmed water of West Bay. Of course, no one wore bathing suits then. Folks just threw their shorts and shirts and shoes in a pile and jumped into the water from the granite outcroppings. There were probably fifteen naked people all swimming at once before dinner. No one brought towels so it meant running around without clothes in order to get skin dry enough to put clothes back on. I did notice that a few lobster boats came closer to shore than usual, but we were all used to swimming naked so no one really paid attention.

After dinner, when most of the people had left and we were cleaning up, my mother said, "They were all naked."

"That's right, Mom," I said. "They were. But they had such a good time, didn't they?"

Clambakes were great for summer, but in the winter we came up with a new way to entertain. One fall we were thinking about what we could do on New Year's that didn't involve staying up until midnight, kissing people we might not even like, and ringing a bell. We considered the idea of having a Chinese dinner party. So we brainstormed and came up with the most amazing and ridiculous ideas. For the previous several days, Bill and I and a few helpers chopped farm vegetables, cut farm meat, made sauces, labeled boxes, wrote out recipes. Almost a hundred people came and spread throughout the whole house.

When it came time to cook, Bill asked all the women to go into the living room and have a drink while the men broke up into teams of three or four. We had about ten stations, each with some kind of heating element; two on the woodstove, two on our apartment-sized gas stove, two on the barbecue outside, two on hotplates, one on an electric frying pan and one Mongolian hot pot on the porch filled with glowing coals. Bill and I had set up a box for each dish containing woks, wooden spoons, vegetables, meats, sauces, oil for frying, chopsticks, all measured and put in jars or bags. On the top was the recipe, spelled out very clearly with instructions for each step.

The men took their jobs very seriously and the women had another drink and could hardly contain themselves they were laughing so hard. The food was fantastic. The men thought they were doing gourmet cooking, and the women, for the most part, got pretty drunk. We had those Chinese dinner parties for several years in a row until they became unmanageable. Everyone wanted to come and the crowd was outgrowing our ten-room farmhouse. I've thought about having another one after a long hiatus but the work involved in preparation makes me shudder. However, it was a load of fun.

We had weddings on the farm. Sara, Amy, Tom, and our dear friend, Wendy. Sara's and Jeff's was the first. It was all farm grown food except for a couple of salmon that I poached and decorated. Even though the heavens opened up just before the ceremony, a quick move to our barn made the wedding a sweet, intimate affair.

Amy and Rich wanted a chicken barbecue so we raised enough chickens to feed over two hundred people. No rain that day.

Tom and Sheila married down at the shore. Because it was after my father developed serious Parkinson's disease, a group of hearty souls picked up his wheelchair and carried it down to the bay with Dad in it. We made Indian food because Sheila is Parsi and her family is from India. Although we bought the fish, everything else was from our gardens.

Wendy and Henri were married with lots of Massachusetts relatives attending, as well as ex-apprentices and friends. Wendy had been an apprentice herself and is a spinner, a good friend, and our medical provider.

The greatest party, especially for Bill, of course, was the Piano on the Porch Party. That first year we wheeled our old ark of an upright piano, creaking and groaning onto the porch. Bill gathered together the best musicians he knew to see if they might be willing to come and play. They all came and they were amazing.

Not your run-of-the-mill hobby musicians, but solid bop players. We sent out cards that said to bring a potluck and spread the word to your neighbors. We usually had over a hundred people, parking their cars in our mown hayfield and walking up the driveway, casserole dish in hand.

Tom Duprey, our trumpet player friend from Massachusetts, had stopped by our farm store one day, said he was vacationing in the area, and Bill said, "Come on up to our Porch Party this Sunday. Bring your horn." So Tom with his trumpet and his wife, Susan, and their two kids arrived and became great friends who came every year to the party and in February to do a coffeehouse gig. The band often had a hand drummer sit in with Bill's congas, or a singer who knew some jazz tunes. They played "A Night in Tunisia," "Have You Met Miss Jones," "Blue Monk," Ella's "Satin Doll," "Tangerine," "Jumpin' with Symphony Sid," and "Billy's Bounce," or better known around here as "Farmer Billy's Bounce." They sounded like something you might stumble across in the Blue Note in New York or the Hi Hat in Boston.

I wonder if the younger generation, growing up with their devices glued to their bodies and living on processed foods, will ever experience the camaraderie of people gathering together to swim naked, eat clams, play music, be part of a new relationship, cook in teams, or just be with each other talking about the world and the neighborhood.

Chapter 15

THE JAZZ GIG

The morning of the gig and the day Tom, the trumpet player, is to arrive, Becky and I make the long trek through the magic tunnel, lugging my rolling suitcase with knitting, my manuscript, and our food for the day. The tunnel seems exceptionally eerie today. I notice the intricately painted doors are ajar, revealing empty rooms I hadn't noticed before. There seems to be more broken furniture in the hallways. But I've never seen any people during the two and a half weeks of hotel/hospital living.

When we arrive, we read the paper and Becky gets me a coffee from the shop down the hall. There's talk of sending Bill to rehab in a couple of days. I still can't imagine him in rehab but at least I know rehab exists. While I wait for Becky, I think about what might be. He could die but he seems to be getting better every day. If he died, I wouldn't be able to cope with the loss. He could do great in rehab and be able to walk haltingly and speak when he could get the right words out. Work the horses? I don't think so. Or he could be a body with a broken mind inside and sit on the porch, watching his horses, listening to the chickens cackle, and shrug, "What the fuck?"

When Becky comes back with coffee, we notice that Bill seems agitated. He flails his arms and legs around as if he wants to get out of bed. We move him back so he's straight and five minutes later he's hanging off the end of the bed again. Every time he moves, his oxygen supply slides to the side and we need to fix it. Tom arrives from Boston early, trumpet in tow. He talks to Bill, takes his hand. I think he reacts but it's hard to tell because he's moving around so much.

Tom mutes his trumpet and begins to play Monk and Dizzy and the Bird. I watch for some recognition from Bill, but it's a stretch. And they're talking about sending him to rehab in two days? Now I'm the one to think "What the fuck?" I want him back. But not like this. I want him back the way he was. But somewhere inside me I know that's never going to happen. He's 82 years old and headed for months of rehab to be able to sit on a porch? Tom plays the whole set for Bill and I listen. Then he plays "Tangerine" for me.

Tom's a great musician and he adores Bill, so it's a bittersweet visit. I see how much love Tom is pouring into his trumpet just for Bill and it makes me smile, a rare thing these days.

"Look how excited he is," Tom says after a particularly restless period where Bill almost throws himself out of the bed. "I'm glad I could play the set."

I'm not so sure that's why Bill is so agitated. Something isn't quite right. He doesn't squeeze my hand when I squeeze his. His eyes are open but they don't look at me. The connection is fraying.

I get word that the coffeehouse has turned into a fundraiser for us. I'm embarrassed. Bill has Medicare and insurance to cover all his medical bills. Mary, from Schoodic Arts for All sends out an email and Facebook notice about the coffeehouse.

"Coffeehouse March 29, Darthia Farm Porch Band All Stars: Jazz at the Hi-Hat. As many of you know, Bill Thayer had an accident and will be unable to perform at the Coffeehouse. Bill would want the show to go on, and the band will be performing with Lynette Woods on percussion. Let's all show our support by attending this performance and joining together to send our best wishes to Bill and Cynthia."

I want to say, "Please don't give us money," but Becky says people want to. They want to help with the hotel bill. They want to do something. Bill is dearly loved in our community. He has been a selectman for many years and our farm is very well respected. The wagons are circling.

I get more than a thousand comments on Facebook when I check yesterday's update. Then I realize he isn't just my husband, he's the whole community's friend and mentor. Every person on the peninsula under 35 has been to tour the farm with the local school's kindergarten and first grade, making cider, riding in the wagon, and learning about growing vegetables and spinning wool. He's Farmer Billy. This is becoming bigger than we are.

I am exhausted. For the first time in two and a half weeks, I leave the ICU during the day to go to the hotel for a nap, but I trust Becky to let me know if I need to come back. She'll be with Bill, centering him back on the bed, adjusting his oxygen. I'm not sure I can make it through the day without lying down. I barely make the schlep through the magic tunnel back to my room where I collapse on the bed. Just an hour. I need this. Just an hour.

And an hour later to the minute, I wake up, startled and anxious. I run back to the ICU, this time with no suitcase in tow. When I burst into the room, Becky seems exhausted, too, from making sure the oxygen is working for him. The nurses see that we have the situation under control, and so rarely enter the room unless we call them, mostly to help move him back to the middle of the bed.

Becky and I set up my MacBook Air to get the live feed from the coffeehouse. Hammond Hall is packed with people and we hear the band tuning up. Tom is there with his trumpet, Don on bass, Rob on piano, Bruce on sax. And at the drum kit is Lynette, the woman I've never seen before, but she knows her bop. Bill is really too agitated to watch it. His body is so restless that every few minutes we have help to move him back to the center of the bed.

"They're going to start soon," I tell him.

Shrug. Shrug.

And then it begins. The quality isn't good. The music and picture fade in and out as we struggle to make it better. We move the computer, tilt it, will it to become clear. Bill continues to flail. Tom the trumpet player thought this morning that the restlessness was excitement over the music but I think something else is going on.

"Look, Bill. There's Tom. Listen."

When the video isn't breaking up, it's amazing. They're all fabulous musicians and can play anything but it shows they all love bebop the best. A few times, Bill glances at the computer. I imagine that he's playing the drums in his mind. But I'm wondering if rehab can help him be able to trade fours.

After a while, the video breaks up so much we can't watch it anymore. I squeeze his hand, our nightly ritual, kiss his forehead, tell him how much I love him, and remind the new nurse to call if there's any change. Becky and I make our way through the magic tunnel back to the hotel. Something isn't quite right but I can't put my finger on it. I plod along the tunnel, pulling my suitcase behind me.

Becky and I make small talk about the weirdness of the magic tunnel; speculate about what might be behind the colorful painted door. We talk about Bill's restlessness.

"I wonder what's causing him to thrash like that," Becky says.

"It's kind of strange. He doesn't seem there today. I wonder where he's gone," I say. "I hope he'll be back tomorrow. He's supposed to go to rehab."

"Let's hope," Becky says.

"He's not out of the woods," I say. "Not nearly."

Chapter 16

A Letter to Bill on His 70th Birthday

On Bill's 70th birthday, we took our children and grandchildren to the island of Carriacou. I wrote this letter to read on that occasion.

"On February 23, 1937, Charles and Barbara Thayer had a miracle baby boy. I call it a miracle because Barbara was never supposed to be able to have any children but found herself pregnant at 40 after giving up on the possibility. Billy was an adorable baby with copious red hair and freckles multiplying as he grew. He was a pitcher on baseball teams his whole youth, went to Derby Academy, and was greatly loved by his aging parents. He got a drum set and was allowed to set it up in the attic of their large house in Hingham, Massachusetts, where he practiced for hours at a time. For a number of years, he took the bus into Boston for his drum lesson and often stopped to sneak a look at the naked women in the burlesque shows on the way to his lesson.

"Billy went to Noble and Greenough School in Dedham, Massachusetts, for his high school years, and senior year, lived in the notorious castle on the grounds, where he had contests with the other lovely boys as to whose spit would hang on the ceiling the longest before it fell to the floor. They had other contests, too, which I would relate if not for the fact that his grandchildren are present. He played hockey and baseball. He drove sports cars in the summer for aging gentlemen. He crewed on sailboats. And he was the drummer for many pick-up dance bands.

"Bill didn't go to Harvard like his father did. Instead he went to University of Vermont to study women, cars, booze, and jazz. He and his roommate used to shoot holes in the bureau with a shotgun just for fun. After a year or two, he was called into the dean's office. 'Sorry, Mr. Thayer, but this is an academic institution and in order to stay on here, you must study.' So poor little Billy went home to Hingham to 'hang out.'

"Whoops! Did I say 'hang out'? Not. Charles, the father of Billy, explained that once one turned 18 and was out of high school,

Bill at 7. No idea whose lamb it was but it certainly was a foreshadowing of events to come.

one had to either study hard and get good grades or go out and get a job. So Bill went to work in an office. And then joined the army because they said they'd send him to language school since he had a penchant for foreign languages. So he went blindly into the armed forces, ready to make his mark on the world.

Me at 7. I may be smiling but I'm not happy with all the fancy clothes. In fact, my cousin, Virginia, and I rolled in the coal bin in protest minutes later and no one was happy.

"Well, Billy has this disease called psoriasis. And it loved the army so much that it took over his poor arms and legs and scalp and bum-bum so badly that he ended up in the hospital. So that was the end of the army—medical discharge.

"The next few years brought a job with his father in Boston as an insurance guy, a wife named Nancy, and three lovely daughters. They all lived in Hingham in a house that they built. Bill bought Amy a little pony named Willow. He worked his way up in the business, played golf on the weekends, and was a young, upwardly mobile guy.

"After a traumatic divorce. he decided to go back to school and do something different with his life. It

was a difficult decision because his parents thought
he should stay in the business but he enrolled at
Bridgewater State College in Special Education and
then completed a Master's in Behavioral Science.
He grew a beard, let his very sparse hair grow long,
played tennis with Dave and Bill, spent time with
the kids on weekends, kept tabs on his parents who
were aging and retired to Cape Cod.

"Bill became involved in anti-war politics, lived
in Reverend Rich's scout house, and joined Dave
England's encounter group and soon after encoun-
tered a beautiful, voluptuous, brilliant woman
named Cynthia. They got married in the church
while their friend Bill Northrup played the raunchy
'Cats on the Rooftop' disguised as a classical piece
on the organ and Tom played and sang a song he
wrote. All five kids were there in adorable matching
shirts as Bill and Cynthia whispered to each other
about people in the congregation that they might
have slept with.

"Cynthia and Bill and the kids went on canoe
trips all around Maine, lived in a tiny apartment
in Bridgewater. Bill had graduated and was getting
his Master's. He taught a very difficult group of
emotionally disturbed children.

"His mother died and his father followed soon
after from a broken heart. Bill, Cynthia, and family,
all moved to an old house in Middleborough, which
they restored to close to its original 1715 condition.
Here Bill picked up carpentry skills and they began
to farm.

"One day he reported that Nancy, his ex,
planned to move to Maine with the kids. 'Oh,

no,' they said. 'What will we do? Duh,' they said. 'What's here that we can't leave? We'll go to Maine, too.' It was an easy decision so they moved to Maine with Tom, Robin, and a menagerie of horses, goats, sheep, and chickens.

"The night before the big move, Bill brilliantly packed the van with chickens so they'd be all ready to go first thing in the morning. Next morning came and—well, let's say the chickens had been busy all night and that the six-hour drive to Maine was aromatic.

"They moved into an old farmhouse with big plans and a big freezer full of the summer's veggies to immediately begin a whole new life. Little Billy now became a great horseman, a stalwart woodsman, a sawyer, a farrier, a John Deere expert, a supreme carpenter. Gone was the insurance man. Enter the rural, agrarian Renaissance man.

"When Cynthia was out of the country visiting her family, Little Billy hauled his dusty old drum set down from the attic where it had been for years, moved the furniture out of the living room and installed his instrument. He became the drummer for several bands—jazz, rock, big band. His skills improved with lots of practice and performance so that now Little Billy is one hot bop drummer.

"Now he's a grandfather and the best grandfather any kid could ever have. And he's still married to Cynthia, who thinks he's the absolutely greatest mate possible. He can still beat just about anyone on the power walk up the big hill and he plays kick-ass jazz.

Gone is the red hair. In fact, gone is the hair. But naked, he looks like a 30 year old.

"Little Billy has grown from a kind, loving, considerate, quirky, handsome little red-headed boy into a kind, loving, considerate, quirky, handsome old man. He has had a great life and has a great life ahead of him. Let's hope we have many more trips to Carriacou."

Chapter 17

SUPPER WITH BECKY

Becky and I have our usual glass of red wine, this time another nice Merlot from a bottle that someone brought into the hospital. We pick through various foods like hummus and guacamole and dates from Colleen and smoked scallops and carrots, gluten-free crackers, some nice hard cheese. It's been a long day and we're back later than usual because of the coffeehouse gig. I awaken the next morning around five, listen to Becky breathe, and think about how lucky I am to have so many generous and thoughtful friends and how lucky I am to be married to the best guy in the world.

It's been two and a half weeks since the accident and there isn't much change. But tomorrow he goes to rehab. It's right in the hospital on a floor above the ICU. I try to picture the rehabilitation process with a man who is thrashing so much they need to put boxing gloves on his hands to keep him from hurting himself or pulling out his IV. It's impossible for me to imagine him getting him on a treadmill or pumping iron. I need to have more faith in the medical team.

Around six, the phone next to my bed rings. I pick up before the second ring. Its Bill's nurse. She says he's had a bad night. *A bad night?* She tries to explain but it's not making any sense to me. I tell her I'm on my way. I wake up Becky, throw some food into the suitcase and leave.

The tunnel seems endless this morning so I pick up my pace. When they moved him so he could have a view of the river, it made for a longer walk. I don't want to run. I'm afraid of falling because I don't feel very strong. I take big walk steps, pass his old ICU with the windowless rooms. I hear Becky behind me. I walk faster, swerve the corner into the ICU with the view of the river. The room is full. Doctors, nurses, respiratory personnel. And a man lies still in the middle of the bed, boxing gloves off, eyes closed, breathing through the trach tube. He has a beautiful face.

The nurse tries to explain. He's had some heart events and they had to use paddles to get his heart going again. Three times. *Wait. He has a DNR order. Do not resuscitate.* But I don't say it. They saved him. I feel tears gathering. I look at him, take his hand. When I squeeze it, he doesn't squeeze back. He's not flailing his arms and legs. He isn't shrugging. He's sleeping. I feel they are all looking at me. I try to ask what happened. I'm not sure I do it well. They talk. Their mouths move and move but I still don't know what they're saying.

Becky asks and they say it again. He had some heart events. But he's in AFib, or atrial fibrillation. I watch the line on the machine. Yes. It looks different. "I'm sorry," the nurse says. I'm not sure what she means by that. I hear them talk but I can't make sense of it. We call Wendy, my dear friend. She has the heart of a friend and the knowledge of a skilled nurse practitioner. She's on her way. We call Sara and Amy. We call Shepsi and Liz. We call Tom and Riley. They're all coming. I sense there will be no rehab. No one mentions it. I stand, unable to react except for the feeling that I am about to cry. I sit down in the chair next to him. One of the brain surgeons kneels down at my level on the floor in front of me and takes my hands in his, like you might to a small child. He begins to move his mouth. I hear him.

He says that Bill has substantial damage from the lack of oxygen to his brain and all the blood inside his skull. His heart isn't strong enough to keep going. The doctor says that because I am the guardian now, I need to make a decision. I look at him. No. He's not there. He's hardly been there since the accident and now he's not there at all. When I fell in love it wasn't with his body, it was with his soul, which seems to have departed. What is left there in the middle of the bed is just his useless body. Where has he gone? My chest feels tight, like my heart is swelling too big for its cavity. Now I know why they say love comes from the heart. I know what my decision is. But I won't voice it until his children come.

People arrive. Shepsi has brought the van in case he needs to bring a body back to the farm for burial. Leila is flying in from New York City. Tom and Riley arrive with Bill's new glasses to replace the ones that still hold the mystery. Sara and Amy arrive. I think Bill knows when they come in and tries to raise his arms to them. Wendy comes in, as do Tom's ex-wife Sheila and her husband Seppy. The room is full. My sister Lisa and her partner Don are on their way from Nova Scotia, a seven-hour ride. Bill needs these people. I need all these people.

"He wouldn't want to live like this," I say. What is "like this"? I look over at him. Does the new "like this" mean lying in a bed not responding to anything? I don't see Bill. I see some man who looks a bit like him, sleeping, with tubes and connections to machines that beep. I know he would never be Bill. Bill died when the accident happened. "We need to let him go," I say to the silent group gathered around us. But I don't look at any of them. I look at the floor instead.

Chapter 18

FINDING CARRIACOU

Bill and I rarely left the farm for the first fifteen years of living here because someone with some farming expertise needed to be here and we felt uncomfortable asking anyone to be that person. The first couple of years vacationing in the Caribbean were not what we wanted but we loved the warmth and the jade-colored sea and the chance to get away for a week or two. We discovered that we didn't like the tourist scene and felt a huge divide between the local people and the tourists.

"I want to go to a warm place where we can get to know the people who live there," I said.

So I bought a guidebook to the Caribbean and searched for a place that we might like to try out. Most were the same old thing. "Lots of activities, private beaches, golf, all-inclusive, massages, swimming pools, night clubs, tennis." Those things didn't interest us. We wanted sun and ocean and friendly people, not a place that fenced out the locals and catered to tourists.

I finally came across a place I never heard of called Carriacou, a small island that is part of the country of Grenada, in the Windward Islands close to Venezuela. The book said, "There's nothing to do there except swim and drink rum and everything is falling apart. But the people have lovely smiles."

"That's where I want to go," I said. "It sounds like a great place."

A few months later, just after Christmas, we arrived in a tiny six-seater propeller plane from Grenada at an airport where the runway was crossed by the main road of the island. They kept people from driving across the runway when a plane was coming in by a flimsy metal gate with a sign that said "Poison Crabs. Do not enter." Of course, everyone knew there were no poison crabs.

The warm salt breeze hit us as soon as we left the airplane. We were picked up by a man with a van that said "Uncle Polo" on the back to go to the Silver Beach Resort. On the way into town, a donkey ridden by a Rasta man with dreadlocks a yard long flying out behind him passed us at a gallop.

Five minutes from the airport, we arrived at the "Resort" and settled into our cabin. I unpacked and pulled to open the drawer of a bureau and the whole front of the drawer came off. *Everything is falling apart.* Then Bill took a shower to get rid of the travel dirt and found there was no hot water.

After we donned our shorts and tees, we walked across a small courtyard to the office to tell them about the water in the shower. We passed a small fountain that wasn't running but was filled with seven large land tortoises. Flowers bloomed all around the main building and the air was sweet from the flowers mingled with spicy from the cooking.

"There was no hot water," Bill said to the woman at the desk.

"No. No hot water," she said in a sweet voice. She looked up and gave us the most glorious smile I had ever seen as she tugged at the large pink flower behind her ear.

"Thank you," Bill said. And we walked back to our cottage.

"We found it," I said. "Why in hell would you need hot water in the tropics anyway?"

"We did find it, Dolly. Let's have a swim."

Bill and me at the beach. We both loved swimming in the warm water and especially loved the warm and lovely people of Carriacou.

Every year since then, for almost twenty-five years, we went to this small island in the Caribbean Sea populated with the friendliest people on earth. The third year, we brought Leila, our granddaughter, who was five or six, and that became a regular trip, every year, at the end of December, just in time to celebrate our anniversary.

Leila was a big hit down there. She was into reciting poetry and entertained folks with a dramatic rendition of Lewis Carol's "Jabberwocky." We took her everywhere with us, laid her down on the floor when she fell asleep. One year, we took her to the community school for a couple of days. The following year, we drove up and let her out to sounds of "Leila's back, Leila's back," from students who remembered her.

When Brianna became old enough to be away from her mom, we brought her. And twice we brought the whole family.

We swam, read books, took long walks to find remote beaches, drank rum punch before dinner, shopped from the ladies selling vegetables on the street, cooked our meals, dragged the grandkids all over the island, and never again went to one of those other islands with beach chairs, crowded bars, and nameless people waiting on us.

Over the years, we experienced amazing moments there. We practically lived in the water, nodding at folks walking along the beach to school or to work. One morning when Brianna was about eight years old, we were at the edge of the waves when she picked up a conch shell. We watched a white tentacle poke out of the opening in the shell, followed by more tentacles and then a small round body. A baby octopus. All white. It slowly made its way up Brianna's arm as we stood in awe of its beauty and the quietness of the moment. Then in a flash, it leapt from her arm back into the water and shot black ink at us through the surf.

Year after year, we made our plans, packed what we thought we'd need, and got on a plane at JFK, and headed for Grenada and then on to the little prop plane to Carriacou.

One year we took a boat with a French family to White Island, not far off Carriacou. The boatman grilled us lobster and made rum punch while we swam in the most amazingly clear water I have ever seen.

As we gathered around waiting for the lobster to be done, one of the young French boys said, "Regardez. Regardez. Les tortues," or "Look. Look. Turtles." We all looked toward him and by his feet a few kiwi fruit–sized baby turtles wriggled out of a hole in the sand and flopped toward the water line. We formed a line with the others to the edge of the waves to keep gulls from swooping down and grabbing dinner.

That year, we watched more than a hundred turtles hatch and helped them get to the sea, made close friends, learned to cook local vegetables, tried fish we had never heard of before, and danced.

A few years later, a new business was holding a Grand Opening party with a string band. We decided to go since it was only a few minutes walk from our "Resort." The meaning of "personal space" is very different down there, something we got used to. Bill and I danced, along with a sea of Kayaks, as Carriacou natives are known, in front of the new store. I've always been a dancer so when a handsome Kayak man wearing a fedora asked me to dance with him, I nodded and joined him in the middle of the street. Immediately, my American personal space was invaded and for a moment I wasn't sure what to do. Then I heard my dad's voice from when I was a child say, "When in Rome!" In Carriacou, dancing is like foreplay and I went with it. He was good looking and had great moves, and I adopted the Carriacou personal space idea, even when he was pressed hard against me. When the music finished, he did a little formal bow and went over to dance with his wife, who had been watching us with a smile on her face.

"That was fun to see," Bill said. And he immediately asked a Kayak woman who seemed like she was alone, if she'd like to dance with him. Halfway through the dance, another woman, very large and voluptuous, went over to them and got behind him and the two of them beat out rhythm with him in between. I've never seen him with such a Cheshire cat grin.

The year we went for Bill's 70th birthday in February coincided with their Carnival, which is three days of a lot of drinking rum, singing, and parading in flamboyant costumes. On one of the days they have what they call Shakespeare Mas, the highlight of the Carnival. Men dress in clothing a Medieval jester might wear with large painted cardboard hoods or capes, each wielding a long switch made from a dried bull's penis. They paired off and began to recite a scene from Shakespeare's *Julius Caesar* in thick

Caribbean accents. One started a recitation from the play until he faltered or made a mistake. Then the other struck him on the colorful hood with the dried bull's penis, making a huge smacking noise and began his recitation where the other left off. As soon as the second one faltered or made a mistake, he received the same treatment and back it went to the first reciter. I was fascinated with the language, costuming, and punishments and got so close that I almost got whacked with the bull's penis myself.

Over the many years of vacationing in Carriacou, we made good friends. Nellie, Clemencia, Reggie, Cuthbert, Shirley, Mary, Endeave, Bubbles. Some came all the way up to Maine to visit us and we were invited to their weddings and birthdays. We loved their smiles, their warmth toward us. Each year our first day on the island was nonstop hugs and greetings when we went downtown to buy our fruits and vegetables. Often I thought of the other islands with their fancy meals and the fancy clothes we were supposed to wear in order to eat the fancy meals and was so glad we had found our little island. And like Maine, everyone waves when they pass by, on foot or in a car, not really a wave, just a hand raised and lowered as they pass.

Chapter 19

THE GREAT ESCAPE

The room overflows with friends and family and medical people all looking to me for guidance. No one contradicts my decision. No one says, "Maybe he'll come around" when I say "We need to let him go." Part of me wants someone to say he might be all right given time. But no one speaks. When I look up, I see the love and kindness radiate from everyone's eyes, including the medical personnel. One of the doctors says calmly they will begin removing his support system. Now we, his friends and family, become his support system.

Bill's nurse comes in solemnly and moves as quietly as if she is gliding on air. Everyone stands back and watches her. She's a dancer. I am stone. She turns off the machine that releases oxygen near his trach tube and pushes it to the side. Slowly and efficiently, she removes his heart stickies and his feeding tube attachment and his IVs. She leaves his trach tube and his stomach tube intact. There is no reaction from Bill. I pray to anyone who might still be inside him that he is comfortable and satisfied that this is the right decision for him.

And gradually, the machines go off, stop beeping and flashing one by one. It takes a long time. She is reverent. She doesn't look at anyone else. She concentrates on Bill. The doctor says that it could be minutes or even hours before his breathing and heart stop. We all watch intently. Curious. Sad. Some tears. But no hysteria. It's like a prayer gathering but without God present. We are sitting in for God here.

Lisa and Don arrive from Nova Scotia. They must have broken all the speeding laws. We greet them and brief them on what is happening. They look ashen and exhausted. They adore Bill and had been visiting for my birthday just two days before the accident. No one knows what to do. Then I hear someone say, "You could crawl into bed with him." I think it's Sara.

I do. I curl right up against him, close my eyes, pretend we are sharing a bed. Well, we are, in fact, sharing a bed. I pretend we're at home in bed and he's holding me gently, like he does. Our intimacy rushes back for a brief moment as I make believe I feel his hand on my side, feel his breath on the back of my head. The room is quiet. I hear my own breathing. His breathing is very loud through his trach tube and seems faster than usual. Perhaps he isn't ready to die yet. He's waiting for something. He's warm against me. I press against him as tight as I dare and I smell his scent. Not the scent of the patient who's been in the ICU for weeks, but the real scent of Farmer Bill who sometimes smells a bit like horse manure.

Because of all the people in the room, I'm hesitant to speak aloud but I send messages to Bill. *Go to the light. It will be fine. I'll be with you. The horses are safe. We'll keep working them. Your grandchildren are growing up to be fascinating human beings. And now we even have a great-granddaughter. I'll be all right, Bill. At least I can cook.* I almost laugh aloud when I think that. *Bill, you have a room full of people who love you. We're waiting with you. Being with you while you die.*

When I think this, I feel tears dripping down my face onto the pillow. I seldom cry but my body takes over and I let it happen. I wonder how long after he dies he will lose his warmth. I lie there with him for an hour. I hear some rustling in the room when people get up and sit down. There is some hushed conversation. It feels holy, reverent, mystical, like the universe is helping us. Then, out of somewhere, comes a voice. "Let's take him home."

Chapter 20

DAD AND THE CALF SHOW

Before my dad died, he came to visit Bill and me every summer, complete with walker, giving my mother a respite from providing his care. I made him oatmeal, poured a swirl of dark molasses over it, drowned it in milk, and set it down on the table next to his coffee. Because of his Parkinson's disease, the sweet milk sloshed over the tablecloth and his pants, splashed down his chin when he brought the spoon to his mouth.

"Dad, it's beautiful outside. We'll take a walk later."

"Yes," he said, spooning another mouthful of the oatmeal through bird lips. It was a juggling act trying to make sure he didn't wander off. Sometimes I raced from the onion garden back into the house to see if he needed help getting to the bathroom. One time I lost him and finally found him in the rhubarb patch with the salt shaker, eating stalks of rhubarb after he'd shaken salt on them.

The back door creaked open and Bill poked his head around the corner. "Tammy Faye. She's starting."

We had been waiting for our black Jersey cow to drop her calf for a few days now. We'd put her in the box stall over a week ago in anticipation.

"What's happening?" my father asked, holding his hearing aid hard against his ear, causing a high-pitched *beep beep*. He was quite deaf and frail from age and disease, but he was still intuitive. He noticed the concern on my face. Each time we had a birth on the farm I felt a mishmash of emotion. I loved the moment when a newborn calf or lamb or kid shakes its head and bleats for its mother, but I could barely stand it when there was a problem—a young animal dying or struggling to survive.

Bill was already back in the barn with the towel he grabbed from the hook. Tammy Faye had birthed several calves and each time produced a healthy youngster.

"The cow is having her calf, Dad," I said.

"The what?"

"The cow. She's in labor."

"I've never seen that," he said. He sipped his coffee without noticing that it was dribbling down his chin and dripping onto his clothes. "I suppose she wouldn't want anyone watching."

"Oh, she's had lots of babies," I said. "She doesn't care."

"I saw a dog have puppies once," he said. "When I was very young. I think they all died."

"Do you want to watch?"

"In the barn?"

"Yes, Dad," I said. "We can't bring her in here."

He laughed. Not a robust guffaw but the small chuckle of an old man. "Is there a chair out there?"

"There will be," I said.

"I'll finish my porridge first."

A brown metal folding chair leaned against the porch rail. I left Dad at the table slurping his breakfast and brought the old chair out to the barn. Bill was already in the stall, forking heaps of steaming dung onto the manure pile and spreading fresh straw around.

"What're you doing with that?"

"Dad's coming out."

"Here? To the barn? To watch?"

"He wants to," I said. I lugged in the dinged-up old chair and set it up. It was a large stall, built to house several head of cattle for the winter so there's plenty of room for Dad and the cow and us. "This a good spot?"

"I can't predict where's she's going to shoot the thing out," Bill said. "But I'll talk to her."

"He'll need help getting over the hump at the entrance," I said.

Dad was in the bathroom when I got back to the house. When he came out, he was all slicked and shined up as if he was going to some charity ball. His hair was parted neatly at his bald spot and drops of water trickled down his temple. His collar was neatly folded against the crewneck of his sweater. He stamped his walker on the hardwood floor ahead of his step each time. The pink wicker bicycle basket adhered to the front of his walker held his eyeglass case, this morning's paper, and a plastic baggie full of oatmeal cookies. He headed for the door. This was serious.

I hovered behind him as we navigated across the yard. Bill stood waiting at the barn entrance to help us over the big step onto the barn floor. Years of horses and oxen moving in and out had dug craters in the wood planking. The barn floor was an obstacle course but we guided Dad through the smoothest part into the large box stall. Tammy Faye stood off to the side, her head drooping low against the new straw.

"Dad, you need to be careful here," I said.

But Dad had his sight fixed on the battered brown metal chair on the far side of the stall. The legs of his walker caught in the straw and Bill had to pull them up each time. We could have used another person. I was terrified he'd fall and break something. A hip. A leg. His confidence.

"When does the show start?" he said.

"It's not a show, Charles," Bill said. "The cow. She going to have a baby."

"Oh, of course. Well, then. I'm ready."

"She's not quite ready," I said. "We have to have patience. It could take a while."

We puttered around the barn while Tammy Faye lay down, got up, snorted, groaned, pawed the straw away from the floor. Dad ate his cookies and read the front page over and over again. After a half hour of obvious contractions with no calf presenting, I slipped into worry mode.

"Look," Dad said. "Seems like a foot is peeking out of that . . . that . . ."

Tammy Faye emitted a loud low groan and there was indeed a single foot protruding. The foot slipped back in. The next time she contracted I was ready to inspect it. Something was wrong. The calf presented upside down, the underside of the chin faced the ceiling. We once had a sheep deliver that way but the books all say an upside down presentation can be tricky. It would take a bit more interference and machismo. We were ready to pull hard on the foot as she contracted.

The calf was large. I could tell from the size of the foot. And it didn't budge when we both pulled. Dad's chair was in perfect viewing position, he'd put down the morning paper, and the bag of cookies had fallen onto the straw. He gaped at the sight.

At each contraction we pulled like hell but nothing moved. Bill walked over to the darkest corner of the barn, pawed through spider webs, and dug into our messy medical cabinet. He came back with a box of old rubber gloves and a jar of Vaseline.

"Dad, the calf has to be turned. It'll be a while. Do you want to go inside?"

"This is a great show," he said. "But I lost the cookies."

"I'll get you some more later," I said.

Between contractions, Bill worked his hand into the cow's vagina, pushed hard against the upside-down head. "Hold her up," he said.

Oh, sure. I was going to hold a 1,600-pound cow up with my little arthritic hands. I grasped the halter and talked to her while Bill was up to his elbow inside, telling her that we were just trying to turn the baby as if she understood English. She moaned low and loud, humped her back, almost squatted on Bill.

"How're you doing in there?"

"Almost got it," he said. When he withdrew his arm I heard a great sucking sound like pulling a body from quicksand. "Should come now."

My father hummed to himself, tapped his foot in the straw. He leaned forward, expecting a new show, better and faster.

The next contraction brought one foot and the tip of the nose, this time right side up. "Didn't get the other foot?"

"Couldn't find it," he said.

The contractions were furious, tide like ripples down her sweaty sides as she pushed at the calf. After a few exhausting minutes, I realized that it was stuck. Why did I bring my father out here? I should have waited until it was almost born, until I knew that everything was as it should be.

Bill left the barn and for a moment, I'm frantic that he'd left me here with an impossibly laboring cow and a father who thought he was at the movies. Bill came back dragging chains like the grim reaper.

"You can't haul out a little calf with those big chains," I said.

"Do you have another suggestion?"

"Well, no." It would be fruitless to attempt to pull the calf out with our hands, slippery on the slimy hock. I nodded. Bill wrapped the chain around its foot.

"If we can just pull it out past the shoulder it'll come fast."

We had had many sheep and goats born with only one foot presenting, the other bent back. The baby's shoulder bone catches on the mother's pelvic bone making it sometimes impossible to push out without help.

We were both almost in Dad's lap as we pulled on the chain when she contracted. "Hope she doesn't lie down," Bill said.

"Oh, is she going to lie down?" Dad asked.

Bill and I waited, the chain slack, for her to contract again. "This time, give it hell," Bill said.

Her eyes widened, her nostrils flared out, and we grabbed the chain, Bill in the front, me just behind, Dad leaning forward in his chair, waving at the end of the chain, trying to grab it.

She groaned, we pulled, Dad clapped his hands at our attempts, we grunted, she swayed. The chain tightened around my wrist but I felt a slight give to it. Bill set his big work boot square on Tammy Faye's rump for leverage and leaned back hard against it.

A pop came from deep inside as the calf released itself and slid to a steaming puddle in the fresh straw. Birth fluids splashed onto Dad's pants. He lifted his foot and touched his toe gently on the calf's back. Tammy Faye took a few steps away from us, broke the umbilical cord, and turned to lick the calf, pulling great sheets of mucus from its nose and eyes.

A queasiness settled in my gut about the problems we might have. The calf might have a broken leg. The mother might have a broken pelvis. But Tammy Faye seemed just fine, took a few more steps, licked hard at the calf's face, pushed at it with her nose to stand. And the calf staggered on its front knees, collapsed into a steaming heap at Dad's feet.

"Come on, you . . . you calf," I said. "Get up."

"Look," Dad said. "The cow had a baby."

Bill flips the calf's leg up and then back down. "Girl," he said.

One more serious shove by Tammy Faye pushed the calf forward again and it lurched to its feet, wobbled a few steps and collapsed. No broken bones. No injuries. Perfectly healthy.

"I think I'll take a nap," Dad said. "All that business made me tired."

We watched a few more minutes just to make sure everything was all right. Bill brought Tammy Faye a bucket of warm molasses water as a treat, to stimulate her lactation and give her energy. I went back to the medical cabinet in the corner for a uterine bolus. She would probably get a serious infection from Bill's hand inside her uterus if not for the antibiotic bolus. It was the size of a man's thumb and brightly pink like Dad's walker basket. I greased up, gently followed the birth canal, dropped the bolus into her uterus, and withdrew my hand.

Dad forgot about his nap. His eyes were wide open, not quite believing what he saw.

When we got back to the kitchen, I washed my hands and made a pot of tea, put a few shortbread cookies on a plate for Dad.

"How was that, Charles?" Bill asked.

"I'd like to go every day," he said. "Is there one tomorrow?"

Chapter 21

HOME

"Let's take him home." *I think* the wise voice is Sara's.

Of course. That's the answer. There's a big cheer from the crowd in the room. We'll take him home. That's where he'd want to be and there's nothing more they can do for him here. That's why he's still alive. He wants to go home. The room becomes a well-oiled machine. This is what I'm good at. I get up and start planning what we need to do. A nurse I hadn't seen before, upon hearing the mention of taking him home, says, "You can't do that. It's illegal."

"No. It's not illegal," Wendy says. Everyone knows what to do.

We gather around Bill's bed and sing "Somewhere Over the Rainbow," à la Ella Fitzgerald. It sounds like angels who are a bit off key.

Back at the farm we have a designated cemetery. We set it up after our little granddaughter, Melissa, was hit by a customer's car. She died at eighteen months old. We will bury Bill there. But if he dies before he gets out of the hospital, we'll have go through a bunch of hoops in order to transport his body back home.

"Hang on, Bill," I say. "You can't go yet. It's not time."

Wendy contacts Hospice. They're on the way. Shepsi says he'll take Bill home in the van. He wants to go to the mall and get a mattress. Shepsi thought he'd be taking home a body, which wouldn't need a mattress. The doctor says that an ambulance would be easier and more comfortable but they say the ambulance isn't available right now except for emergencies and could take a while to arrive. Becky calls Ray, a friend of Bill's, and one of the town fathers, Jim, who is another dear friend, and finally Tate, Jim's brother and our town fire chief—no small feat considering it's late on a Saturday evening.

"Tate, Bill's dying and we want to bring him home," Becky says. "Is the town ambulance available?"

"It's on the way," Tate says. "No charge. Not for Selectman Bill." Gouldsboro is about an hour and a half away and it's a foggy night. I know they'll be here as soon as they possibly can.

Tom and Riley will go back to the farm to help get ready. Tom's ex-wife Sheila, the mother of Leila and Brianna, and her husband Seppy will also head back and get a room ready for him. Bill still sounds strong and looks calm. He's not dying yet. Hospice arrives and writes prescriptions for morphine to make him comfortable. Sara and Amy head off to get the drugs. Lisa and Don head off to my hotel room to pack my things. I warn her about the magic tunnel but she doesn't seem concerned. Wait until she sees it!

My job? I go over to Bill. "You are going home, Bill. Home." Bill reacts in the strongest way I've seen since he came into the ICU. He knows. He throws his hands up, as if to say, "Hurrah! Now get me home so I can get on with this dying business."

I've been updating followers every day on Facebook but I haven't for couple of days. They'll know something has changed. Those of us who remain wait impatiently for the Gouldsboro ambulance to arrive to bring Bill back to the farm to die. Wendy goes down to Emergency to meet them and show them to the room, quickly. Each person has a job to do and it's working like clockwork.

I have a moment of panic, thinking that perhaps I have made the wrong decision. Then I picture us sitting on the porch again, watching someone else drive Star and Andy pulling the wagon. I rush down the corridor to see if the ambulance is here yet. And then back to the room. He is still breathing. "Bill, hang on just a little longer." The hospital staff is in awe of what we are doing, the sheer power of it, the number of people involved. They stand back and let us do what we need to do. The hospice nurses explain how the drugs should be administered and what to expect, but Wendy knows already.

Bill's breathing seems to slow a bit. *Please don't die yet,* I whisper to myself. That would mean mountains of red tape, involve the morgue, take hours and hours. And it's a weekend. No. It's settled. He's going to hang on until we get him home. The wonderful volunteers who operate the ambulance have arrived with the gurney. I rush in to tell Bill. "They're here. They've come to take you home." I grab his hat from the table beside my chair and lift his head so I can position it.

Things move quickly. They have to. The ambulance drivers transfer him in one effortless swoop to the gurney, strap him in. We sign paperwork, talk a little more to the hospice people. Everything is a go. Leila will drive my car home. Someone brought it to the hospital days ago. I have no idea where it is but she says she will find it. I follow the gurney down the long corridor toward the waiting ambulance. We don't have to go through the magic tunnel this time.

"If he dies," I say to the drivers, "Just pretend he's still alive. Just talk to him and keep going." And they do. We pass guards and I say, "We're almost there, Bill," as if he's going to respond.

"Not much longer, Bill," the man who's at the head of the gurney says to him.

"Just keep going." I say to the volunteer ambulance drivers. We're almost to the ambulance.

Chapter 22

THE DEATH OF MELISSA

Cucumbers

You stood defiant
on your sturdy brown feet
holding fast the cucumber
snatched cleverly from my full basket.
"Did you take Nana's cucumber?" I said.
You turned, gripping the treat in your small hand
and toddled along the stones
away from my grasp.

Hours later but in another time
when everything has changed,
I help your mother wash your still flesh
and when we get to those brown feet
I think that I can't continue.
But we wipe gently over your toes
with the warm cloth,
pour out the lavender oil onto your
hard belly.

Melissa was a high-spirited, musical toddler, always moving, dancing, stealing cucumbers. The day was September 4, 1996. I was canning peaches. Bill had taken a beef critter to the slaughterhouse. Melissa bolted out the kitchen door. Sheila, her mother, went out after her. I continued peeling and cutting the peaches we had bought from a farm in Blue Hill when a few minutes later, Sheila came into the kitchen carrying Melissa.

"Call 911," she said. She laid Melissa on the floor while I ran to the phone on the wall. "There is no 911 here," I said. I read the number for the clinic at the top of our phone list and dialed it.

"There's been accident. It's Cynthia from the farm. We're bringing her in." They asked a few questions and I answered. Questions like how old she was and what the injuries might be.

"I'll drive," I said.

Sheila carried Melissa to the car and an apprentice who was helping with the peaches came along. Melissa wasn't moving. I drove as fast as I safely dared. About halfway there, I got stuck behind a car that was crawling along. I put on my blinking lights and leaned on the horn until she pulled over and I passed her, speeding to the clinic. Every time I pass that spot on the road, I see that car, poking along.

We arrived and I drove around the back of the building. They were waiting for us. Sheila carried her in where she was taken by the doctor to an examining room. We waited in another room for what seemed a long time. Tom came in, frantic. We paced. It seemed like ages before they came out with the news. There was nothing they could do. They were sorry.

Tom was hysterical. He threw chairs. They closed the clinic, cancelled all the patients, and we were there alone with the doctors, nurses, and Melissa's body. We said we wanted to bring her home and bury her on the property. Between Dr. Crowley and Eve at the town office, we got all the permissions and deemed

Bill and me with Melissa August 4, 1996. Melissa was a happy child, musical and impish. Comical like her sisters. We all loved her a whole heap.

a small plot of land to be the Darthia Farm Cemetery. Bill found out when he returned home from the slaughterhouse to find police blocking the bottom of the driveway, keeping people from coming up.

News spread fast and the community circled around us. Some finished canning the peaches; others helped Sheila dry up her milk because she had been still nursing Melissa. A couple dug a grave. Others brought food. Lots of food to feed the people who would be here, helping, consoling, grieving.

We buried her on the farm, wrapped in a white sari that my grandmother had brought over from India at the start of the 20th century, which was the appropriate thing to do since Sheila's Parsi family had come from India. Melissa's parents were both musicians so it was also appropriate that they played The Allman Brothers' "Sweet Melissa" on the day of the burial. Tom and Sheila carried her wrapped body out of the house to that music as people gathered.

Soon after the burial, friends brought plants and created a beautiful garden near the grave, filled with perennials, and ringed with stones. A friend carved MELISSA into the top of a granite bench. Sheila's family arrived from California and mine from Nova Scotia. A very sad day for everyone, but for Sheila and Tom it was life changing. And to this day I can't eat a canned peach.

Her sister, Leila, was only four when Melissa died but she understood what had happened, although she thought that she was somehow responsible for Melissa's death. That's very hard to explain to a child. But Sheila was an amazing mother and somehow we continued to live our lives, although Melissa is still on all of our minds; Tom's, Sheila's, Leila's, and even her sister, Brianna, who was conceived after Melissa's death.

September 4, 1997

It has been a year today
since your mother carried your still
body into the kitchen,
A year since we brought you home to bury.

Today is the day to take down
your sundress from the clothesline,
to erase the telephone message
with your laughter in the background.
Today I gave your mother the bag
of bloody clothes that I kept
hidden under my bed,
kept to touch and smell when I was alone.

What will I touch now when I want
to have you close?

Tomorrow I will dump the colored paper clips
all over the coffee table
and, for a moment, imagine that you spilled them.

Chapter 23

THE RIDE HOME

Although he isn't responding much, I feel he knows what we're doing and why. When I touch his hand, I feel something back. I talk to him all the way out to the ambulance. When we get outside and the doors open, one of the drivers says, "You go right in this door and you can sit beside him."

The air is fresh and smells a little like the river. It's been two and a half weeks since I've been outside, since I've stepped on the ground, since I've been away from the stuffiness of the hospital. The ambulance attendant opens the door and I take my seat while they slide the gurney into the back. She sits in back with me while her partner sits in the driver's seat. The air is *thick-a-fog*, as they say here, so the going is slow. If he dies now, it's OK because we're out of sight of the "powers that be." But he hangs on. When I speak he moves a hand or his head, or his foot wiggles. "Home. Bill, we're going home," I say over and over.

The woman chats about Bill, the weather, Gouldsboro town politics. Her voice is soothing. We huddle close together beside Bill in the dark ambulance and I feel her kindness, her concern.

I'm not in a rush this time. The driver is taking it slow and that's fine. I know he won't die until he gets home.

"How does he seem?" I ask.

"He's stable," she says. "He's going home."

When we turn into our drive, I change my line. Now it's "We're home, Bill, you're home." I say it all the way up the bumpy driveway. I jump out of the ambulance to make sure everything is ready for him. What has happened is incredible. Sheila and Seppy have moved his high hat, bass drum, snare drums, cymbals, from the middle room into our spare room and replaced it with a lovely twin bed, all made up. There's nothing else in the room except for Bill's wing back chair in the corner. We had requested a hospital bed from hospice but there's a message on the answering machine saying they are stalled in Waterville and won't be able to come due to the fog.

I rush out to the dooryard to tell the ambulance folks the room is all ready for him. They open the back doors of the ambulance and pull out the gurney, wheel it toward the farmhouse door. Bill looks peaceful and is breathing through the trach tube with an even breath.

"Hi, honey. You're home."

But the gurney won't fit around the corner into the kitchen. They try several ways but it just won't work. They check the back door but it's too dark and the ground too unstable to push the gurney all the way around to the back of the house. "We'll carry him in," someone says. It's a sweet moment. Someone laughs and it's infectious. After all, it's a funny situation. A few of the men along with the ambulance folks pick him right up from the gurney. He doesn't weigh as much as he did a few weeks ago. It's gentle and loving, the carry. He still wears his hat but the only other thing he has on is his hospital gown that gapes in the back. Bill relaxes and they easily bring him in, past the woodstove, past the kitchen table, into the lovely room where he practiced his drumming.

Everything is in place. The drugs, the drug schedule, hospice, the family, the bed. They tenderly lower him down onto the pillow as if he were a small child who had fallen asleep during a party and needed to be put to bed, and place a sheet on him. And when I didn't think it would be possible to get more loving, thoughtful, and organized, in comes a mattress from our little seasonal BnB, which is quickly placed on the floor right beside his bed. It's for me.

Chapter 24

LIFE, LOVE, DEATH

When I was a young teenager, I often wondered about the
meaning of life, love, and death, but since I was 16, I've been too
busy living life to think about any of it. I remember summering
in New Hampshire with my aunt, going out into the meadow
behind the house, lying down in the wild flowers, and looking
at the sky. I thought hard about living and dying; I wondered
what dying would be like and imagined how terrible it would be
if one of my parents died. At that time. I was trying to decide if I
believed in heaven and hell and, as I looked at the sky, deciding
whether I really wanted to be up or down. It seemed to me that
heaven might be very boring but hell could be painful at best.

But now that I'm in my dotage, I've caught myself mulling
over what it means to say, "I love you," to another person. I guess
it depends on the relationship. A child's love for a mother is very
different from a mother's love for a child, for instance. My family
didn't say those words very often. It's kind of a new thing. I
remember hearing "I love you" only in an occasional movie.

Sometimes when I say " I love you" to someone, it really
means that I still care about them and enjoy their company, or
I'm sorry they are going through a hard time. Saying it seems like
a touch when a touch isn't possible, such as on the telephone or
in an email. When Bill and I make the "I love you" sign to each

other, it feels like a touch that we don't quite follow through on, which makes it somewhat titillating. Like holding back during sexual encounters.

Then sometimes I think love just means a strong friendship, with something else going on like a sexual attraction or a long history of a relationship with that person. Then sometimes it means that I love truffles and scallops or I love driving. No strong relationship there. Or how about this? "I love your new friend." Just met the person. No relationship. No history. No blood connection. No common DNA. Just a few minutes of chatting at the door.

So I now find it impossible to determine whether I love someone or not. It seems that human beings, as opposed to other animals who live in the moment, need to expound upon everything like life, love, and death, to make it a bigger event than the natural evolution of human existence.

Love is a way that nature ensures the continuation of the human race. Plants and animals procreate, so that the species continues. Love makes sure that happens when it comes to humans, producing feelings of lust that make you want to get physically close to another person in order to procreate. And death guarantees that we always have young ideas influencing our lives and that we aren't inundated with so many old people that there isn't room for the young ones coming up.

I believe we are all part of the grand scheme of Mother Nature and that means we need to be born, live, love, and die in order to make it all work. Yes, it's tragic when a young person dies due to an accident or illness or other reason, before he or she has been able to experience what the world offers. And no one is to blame for most deaths. It's just part of the scheme of things. We, as humans, then struggle to live our lives without that person. We miss them. We wish they hadn't died. We yearn for just one more word, one more touch, just one. But we keep going and going as living without them eventually becomes somewhat easier.

When someone dies, I believe the only things left are the memories of that person, which can create illusions that at times seem real. But, although death is very sad, I believe someone who dies is no more. Everything you might have loved about them is gone and disintegrating. Memories are all that's left of the look on their face, the feel of their skin, their smell, the sound of their voice. We humans don't really want to accept death, which is why we create an afterlife where our loved ones go after they die and where we can join them when we die. Almost all races and tribes of people have a myth about where one goes after death.

Chapter 25

THE GATHERING

After Bill's settled in his bed and morphine swabbed onto his cheek by his girls, we begin the "rally around" part. The wine comes out. There's food. More people come. Becky calls her husband, Arthur, her son Brendan, and his wife Candace, who is very pregnant. They all arrive. Liz from down the lane comes up. All the players in the "great escape" are still here. We light candles, pour more wine, pass around plates of food that people have brought. The house is full. People tell stories. And then the horrible, wonderful part. We start to sing.

It sounds horrendous as we are all belting out the words in different keys because we have something to say and want to be heard. Funny thing is that most of us are musicians of some sort and would never sound like that in another situation. We sing "Over the Rainbow," and "What a Wonderful World," and then the choices disintegrate into "Zip-A-Dee-Doo-Dah" and "Farmer in the Dell." We pour each other another round of wine and sing louder. No one is drunk but we're all bit lightheaded from the wine, the company, and the day's events.

Then I remember one of my favorite poems, Frost's "Death of the Hired Man," which I insist on bringing out. Seppy reads it and it is very poignant and appropriate.

Left to Right Amy, Bill, Alison, and Sara. Bill was a wonderful dad and amazing and playful grandfather.

Wendy keeps a keen eye on Bill to make sure he's getting enough morphine and that he's comfortable. Bill opens his eyes a few times and I see a twinkle there. I'm not one for touchy-feely stuff but love is heavy in the room. It seeps into all the corners and settles around Bill. I can almost see it. It's a fabulous evening with friends and family. And we each have a job to do. Mine is to be loved and cared for. Not my usual, but I'm going with it.

After a raucous evening, we settle in for the night. We all think this will be it. He'll die before morning. The house is full of people who are spending the night. Sara and Amy; our granddaughter, Leila, who flew in from New York; Wendy, who will help with any medical issues; my sister and Don. Wendy sleeps on Bill's chair in case he becomes restless and needs more morphine. I sleep in the comfortable memory-foam bed right next to Bill. His breath is fast but even. He doesn't move except to breathe. I awaken a few times but sleep fairly well, which astonishes me.

In the morning, everyone gets up early. Bill is still alive. Perhaps he wants another party. We administer more morphine. I need to put something on Facebook or people will be showing up at the hospital. I send it out to the email list and put it on Facebook.

> March 31
> Hello all,
> There have been some developments in Bill's condition that we'd like to keep private for now. He is at home with family. We will send an update, but right now, we just want to thank you for the unflagging love and support you have sent Bill. We cannot express how grateful we are for that gift.

Immediately people respond. Hundreds of them. "I'm sorry," was the most common.

"I'm so sorry. I'm so glad he's at home."

"I'm sorry. He gave it hell, didn't he?"

"I'm sorry. Please tell me when I can help."

Everyone knows what the message means. One of our early apprentices and a skilled carpenter, Jeff, calls to say he his making a wooden coffin, which will be ready the next morning. Liz comes in with Bill's vest that was sliced down the middle during the medical crisis; it has been mended, carefully and perfectly, by the spinners. Susanne made a little pocket where there had been a tear. Susan made a crocheted totem, which lies in another new pocket. You can barely notice the jagged line up the front where scissors slashed it. I lay it on his chest over the "Home" tee shirt that our nephew, Josh, gave him for Christmas. We put cool cloths on his forehead and stroke his hands. And he breathes on through the trach tube, which makes the breathing sound louder.

Get-well cards arrive. Becky calls Jason, the town's sand and gravel man, to see if he'll be able to dig Bill's grave in our small cemetery. He'll do it tomorrow morning. No charge. Food arrives from community folks who cook and bake when someone is ill or has died. Soup from Mary, lobster salad from a fisherman's wife, loaves of freshly baked bread, pecan squares from Sheila. We need the food—so many people to feed.

Everyone talks to Bill—

"You're home now, Bill," and

"Hi Buppa, it's Leila," and

"Brianna's on her way."

There is no sign of Alison or any of her children coming over to say good-bye, but I guess I shouldn't have hoped for it. It's too late for Bill, but I thought it might help Alison and her girls find some closure for their decision to stop connecting with us and to refuse to tell us why.

Each time someone says "home" I see a small flicker of life from him. He knows he's home and that we all love him to pieces.

The women from hospice arrive. They seem very kind but very professional. They check him to make sure he's comfortable, check his blood pressure and heart rate, look at his skin, and say it won't be long. Everything is slowing down and he probably won't live through the night. We make preparations. Someone finds out that Hammond Hall is free on Saturday in case we want to have a service there. Don and some of the others clear out an area in the overgrown cemetery in preparation for Jason's arrival with the backhoe. It's a strange combination of elation and grief, not anything I would have expected in this situation.

Shepsi comes in with his adorable four-year-old, Cedar, who wants to see his friend, Billy. Shepsi's daughter, Harbor, who is seven, isn't up to coming. Cedar seems very comfortable with it all and is happy to see that Bill is getting such great attention. He pats his hand and talks to him quietly.

Amy leaves and goes to Alison's house, which is just a few miles away. She'll catch a ride to Bangor where her husband will pick her up. She needs to take care of her dogs. I struggle to understand Alison's inability to say good-bye to her dad and feel a sense of compassion for her sisters. A few people come up the driveway but are politely sent away. It's a surreal day. We're all waiting for something we don't want to happen but there's no alternative. That night, when we go to bed, we know it's the last night, that in the morning, everything will be changed. I'll be a widow. I'm not sure I know how to do that.

Chapter 26

THE BARN FIRE

I had been teaching for Maine Writers and Publishers Alliance that May 10, 2012, up in Maine lake country. I got home around suppertime to find Bill finished with chores and waiting for me on the porch with our new puppy, Kelpie. I poured a glass of red wine and sat down next to him to watch the sunset, which was particularly beautiful that evening. We had a new couple on the farm as apprentices and Bill said the guy was a bit pushy and had changed all the plans Bill made about housing the chicks that had just arrived. I went out to take a look and thought they were kind of crowded and the heat lamp was a little too close to the hay floor. I should have insisted on changing the setup but I didn't.

"I missed you," I said when I came back to the porch. "But it was a great time. Very good students and an amazing place, right on the lake."

"Good. Not much happening here. The new guy? Not too sure about him."

"Maybe we should talk to him in the morning," I said.

We went to bed early and shortly after midnight, Bill woke me up, panicked. "I think the barn is on fire." He jumped out of bed and pulled on some clothes, looked out the window. "Oh, God." And he ran downstairs.

I had a nightgown on so just ran after him without changing except for slipping my feet into my old Crocs. On the way out, I grabbed the phone from the wall and started calling 911. "Our barn is on fire. Please come quick."

"I'll notify them right away," the woman said.

I hung up because there were things to do. There was no sign of Bill but I thought he'd probably gone to the back of the barn to get the horses out. Flames were licking out of the windows and up into the cupola. Then I saw the sheep. They had an enclosure just off the barn and some were outside. Our best sheep had just birthed three beautiful ewe lambs who were lying down near the barn. I couldn't tell if they were sleeping or dead. Then one of our old ewes ran toward the fence, bleating. Her back was on fire: flames shot up into the air. The sheep had been sheared but they had an inch or two of wool that had grown back. The ewe ran back and forth, frantic to escape the flames crawling up the back of her neck.

I ran to the gate and struggled to open the latch. The heat was intense but the ewe's screams were forcing me to try. I held my nightgown up to my face because of the heat and continued my attempt to get close enough to open the gate and let her out. I tried so hard but the heat was just too much. All I could think of was Joan of Arc, one of my childhood heroes. I failed. I backed away from the gate and watched her circle the enclosure, flaming, until she dropped.

No fire engines. No police. I called 911 again and again. "They'll be here as soon as they can." I know they're all volunteers but the fire station is only three miles away. It seems like it's been hours since I called them but I know it hasn't been long. By that time Ivelisse, our gardens manager, had joined me. I called 911 again but then heard the sirens coming closer. "They're coming," I yelled into the phone before I hung up. By then the new apprentices were awake and moving cars away from the house.

Our son Tom, who lived just down the hill, arrived. He'd seen the flashing lights from the fire engines and the flames shooting from the cupola.

Ivelisse and I sat down on the grass. She was hysterical and I was hysterical inside trying to hold it together in case I needed to do something important. Then we heard it. "Peep, peep, peep." It went on and on and on. We looked around but couldn't see anything. The firemen were spraying their hoses, the place was in chaos. But the "Peep, peep, peep," continued and became louder and more incessant.

"Oh, my God," Ivelisse said. "Look! It's a little chick." She grabbed it and held it close to her. It must be one of the chicks that hatched a couple of days ago. There were four or five of them living underneath the mother hen in the barn.

Bill staggered out from behind the barn. "It's too late," he said. "I can't get near them." Tears streaked through the soot that was smeared over his face. One of the EMTs came to check to see if we were all right. She took one look at my face, which was starting to blister, and brought me into the ambulance to dress the burn.

The barn was an inferno. Four hundred bales of hay fueled the fire and we knew nothing could live through that. The barn was full. Three horses, pigs, calves, sheep, ducks, chickens, and our old cat, Booger. Everything was in danger. The outside walls of the house felt hot. The picnic cooler on the porch was melting. I ran into the house and grabbed the hard drive from the computer and took it far out back to the garden shed. I was trying to save all our farm information and photos.

The firefighters saw how upset we were. "My guess is, Bill, that they died of smoke inhalation before the fire got to them," one of them said.

I looked over at the old ewe, burned to a crisp, and realized that it wasn't true for all the animals. I prayed that the horses died fast from the smoke.

Bill was ashen. His cherished horses. Gone. Two of them he had raised from young colts, trained them, loved them, worked with them every day. He would have died to save them, but there was no saving. The fire was too advanced.

We were up all night, of course, trying to help any way we could. I fell several times in my rush to get from one place to another, so my nightgown was coated in mud. The firefighters did what they could but they told us there was nothing left to save, so they turned their hoses on the house and the store, which were in danger of igniting. When the firefighters felt they could do no more and the barn site was burned down to smoldering, they left with their trucks.

By then it was daylight and everyone on the farm was gathered around our kitchen table, me still in my nightgown with a large bandage over one side of my face. Ivelisse held the small chick she now called Lucky, who snuggled close to her. We talked about what to do. It was too soon. But we all agreed that we couldn't rebuild a wooden post and beam barn like the old one. Maybe something small, pre-fab metal.

The new couple planned to go into Ellsworth to get something they needed. "Could you go to the feed store?" Bill asked. "I'm out of medicine for Gus."

He burst into tears. Gus had died in the fire. It was heartbreaking to see Bill's anguish over losing his old horse that he raised from a colt. I would have given anything to have helped him in that moment but there was nothing to do or say.

As we sat in silence, allowing Bill to sob quietly in his chair, there was a knock at the door. Then the door opened. It was one of our customers from the nearby town of Corea. She and her partner often came to buy tomatoes or some pesto for dinner.

She carried an envelope in her hand and was weeping so that she couldn't speak. She passed me the envelope, gave me a hug, and left, closing the door gently as if in slow motion. I held the envelope for quite a while before I opened it. Inside were fifty crisp one hundred dollar bills. Five thousand dollars in cash from someone we knew only as a customer. I held it up. I couldn't speak. I passed the bulging envelope around the table.

"This is meant to tell us something," Bill said.

"We need to rebuild," I said.

The only animals we had left were the laying hens because their coop was far enough away from the barn to escape the flames, and one little peeping chick named Lucky. The thought of starting over was daunting, but the faith of the woman who came with the envelope made us think we could really do it. We made plans, decided what kind of barn we wanted. Our neighbor down the road came up to say he wanted to be the contractor and he'd like to do it for free.

We broke ground on the new post and beam barn, set back a few feet from the last barn's footprint and a little taller, but otherwise very much the same. We received money and letters from all over the country, hoping we would rebuild. Linda, one of the spinners, a minister in her other life, volunteered to come often and help keep track of the finances so that I could thank everyone.

The children at the local school made and sold little bracelets and sent us cash in an envelope; Maine Writers and Publishers Alliance sponsored an event in Portland where writers came and sold their autographed novels and memoirs as a fundraiser. Hammond Hall had a public supper. Maine Organic Farmers and Gardeners Association gave us lumber, Johnny's Selected Seeds replaced carts and other equipment that we lost. Liberty Graphics printed twenty tee shirts with our logo on the front and

Bill and I holding the new horses, Andy and Archie, in front of their new home built by our loving community.

"I helped rebuild Darthia Farm" on the back. A farmer who raises sheep nearby promised us a flock of sheep from his island.

When the crew arrived to begin building the new barn, people from the area brought table saws, ladders, hammers, and loads of macaroni and cheese to keep the crews going. Lucky grew some bright feathers and we soon realized he was a rooster. He never left Ivelisse's side. She brought him to school to meet the children and he became the symbol of renewed hope in the life of the farm. The miracle of it all was that we received almost to the dollar the amount needed to rebuild the barn and replace the lost animals. In October 2012, we moved in the new flock of island sheep and Bill went to Kentucky to bring back the new Haflinger team, Andy and Archie, which I had found online. When we read the registration papers that came with Andy, we saw he was a first cousin to old Gus who perished in the fire.

It didn't take long to break in the new barn, to dirty the spotless barn floorboards with mud and manure to make them look more barnlike. We bought harness, equipment, medicines for the animals, a new notebook to keep the island sheep records straight. A friend on Mount Desert wanted to buy us a sheep, so we contacted a woman who raises Coopworths and our friend bought a beautiful black Coopworth ewe who had triplets every year after that.

We were back in the farming business thanks to the kindness of our community and beyond. The sign at the top of our driveway now reads, "Rebuilt by Human Kindness."

Chapter 27

DEATH WATCH

Wendy and I settle in for the night, Wendy again sleeping in Bill's wing chair. I lie in the comfortable BnB bed beside him. There is no sleeping for me. I breathe with his breath, just to get close to him. The house is very quiet. No party tonight.

Sometime in the late night, Bill's breathing becomes fast and loud. It stirs me from my thoughts about midnight and I reach up to touch his hand, tell him he's home, and that everything is all right. There's no response except for the labored breathing. He's had his morphine so he's not in pain. I listen to the breathing without speaking, waiting for it to stop. Wendy doesn't speak, but I know she's awake and listening, too. With each breath, I expect there won't be another. It goes on and on and I wonder where he is getting the energy to continue. I whisper to him. "Go to the light, Bill. It's OK."

I think about all the things we've been through during our forty-five years of marriage. Melissa's death. The estrangement from Alison. The barn fire.

My memories are full of color, as vivid in their reality as Bill's dying. I remember the good times, too. The community helping to rebuild the barn and get us back in business. The births of the grandchildren, all those wonderful parties at the shore, the trips we made to Carriacou and Paris, the wonderful caring relationship we had with each other.

I'm not sure how long he can keep it up, but he does for several more hours. Eventually, the breaths are a little farther apart and I know it's coming. After each breath, I think it's the last, but then he takes another.

"Bill, you gave it hell," I say. "Now you can let it go. It's all right. I'm helping you go."

Death. I want to talk to Wendy but I'm afraid she might be asleep. I wait, amazed that he can continue in such a labored state. And then it happens. There is no more breath.

Chapter 28

A FEW OF THE THOUSAND MESSAGES AFTER BILL'S DEATH

"Farmer Bill welcomed me as apprentice at Darthia Farm, way Downeast on the rocky coastline of Maine. Bill worked the land with his draft horses and played drums in his jazz band until just last week, and he was buried by family and friends on the soil that he stewarded this morning. Pretty much everything practical and meaningful I know how to do in this world—how to make pie crust and build a compost pile, when to harvest garlic and how to braid it, how to cut potatoes for planting and to can blueberries for jam—I learned at Darthia Farm. I might have passed through Bill's life, apprentice #100, part of a decades-long commitment to teaching, but his wisdom, self-discipline, kindness and high expectations all had a profound effect on me, and I will be grateful

Bill sleeping at Schoodic. He was skilled at taking cat naps, especially in the barn, in the hayfield, and by the ocean.

forever to him and to Cindy. What a life well lived."

"Bill taught me to wield a chainsaw, milk a cow, slaughter turkeys, and layer compost piles. By example to face challenges with grit and integrity; to walk gently on this precious earth. Henri and I were married at the farm thanks to his and Cynthia's generosity, and our daughter Hannah Rose spent a good deal of her childhood there. We were all enriched by being in his light. Soar high, dear Farmer Billy."

"The tears that are shed now validate a life lived and loved. They make way for smiles of uncounted memories."

"Soon the tight wraps of grief will unfold like the many blossoms of spring and a flood of beauty and love will flow with the lingering tears."

"I'll never forgot the week I spent on the farm with you both. Early mornings with Bill Thayer to feed the chickens, let out the horses, etc., then on to the gas station for a coffee and back home for a breakfast of fresh eggs."

"I have been pretty angry at a lot of old white men as of late. It's a damn shame to lose one of the good 'uns."

"Bill was the kind of soul that just brought a calm while in his presence."

"I can't think of a life better or more honestly lived. What a generous, interesting, kind, and true-to-self human."

"May he be accompanied by angels to wherever his next life takes him."

"My prayers goes out to his family, us here at Ray's Meat Market will miss his smiling face. He was a great man and farmer."

"I'll miss that twinkle in his eye. I am so sorry. Hugs to you."

"Hearts are breaking all over the planet today."

"Truly one of the most authentic souls I have known."

"There have been a few people in my life whose passing has felt like the fall of a great tree in the landscape. Bill is one of those huge presences."

"Always a gentleman, kind and caring to those who knew him."

"Tomorrow we will work harder to create the world Bill Thayer would want us to have."

"A beautiful heart, a beautiful soul, a beautiful man."

A friend who is a stoneworker, Joe Auciello, carved these words into a granite bench we already had.

"I will miss seeing him at the transfer station."

"He was a shining light. And I can honestly say I will spend the rest of my time thinking, what would Farmer Bill do?"

"Rest in peace, old Farmer Bill. Dizzy and his horn are waiting for you."

Chapter 29

AFTER DEATH

Wendy and I lie quietly for a while before we talk to each other about what happened. It's early morning and we are the only ones awake. I feel that if we talk about it, or even recognize that I am not sleeping, I will have to face the reality of it all.

"I can't believe he kept that up for so long," Wendy finally says.

I can't either. He didn't want to leave. He was so strong. Perhaps he was waiting for another raucous singing and wine party. We wake the others. I talk to him when no one else is in the room, say things like, "We had a good run of it," and "Can't imagine who else would have put up with me." And of course, "I love you," even though I'm still not really sure what that means. Does it mean that I'm sad when he dies? Or that I'll miss the intimacy of his body? Or that I'd do anything in the world for him? All those things are true. But what does love really mean, anyway?

As people pass through the drum room they touch him, touch me, say quiet utterings. Someone makes scrambled eggs for those who are hungry. The mood has changed from the elation of the singing to a quiet respect for what has happened in our midst.

I begin what I'm best at. Organizing. "I need to make a list," I say.

"Not yet," Sara says. "It's not time yet."

She's right, of course. Sara knows when things should be done or said. I'm immediately sorry for starting to organize so quickly. It's not the right thing to do. But I can't sit still. I'm afraid of my emotions, afraid that I won't be able to hold up and get things done. I respect Sara so much for being able to do what she feels. I look at her face. She loves her dad with such a pure heart.

Sara asks if I have any sage. "I do. It's in the garden just out-side the back door," I say. "It's still good even after all the snow."

She goes outside to our herb garden and comes back in with a bunch of sage, which she ties with a string. She methodically opens the window behind her father's body and lights the sage bundle, which begins to smolder. "This will help his soul leave so he won't be wandering." She waves the smoking sage back and forth and across Bill's body for quite a while until she feels it has done its magic. The sweet scent of the smoldering sage fills the room. I'm in awe of Sara's strength.

Jason, the backhoe operator, arrives and someone brings him down the lane to our small lonely cemetery and digs a hole—with lots of help clearing and deciding on the spot, I imagine. Don is in charge of the cemetery. He says Jason hit bedrock but the hole is four feet down so we give the OK.

Wendy has been talking to the doctor from her clinic about the death certificate. The house is full of people and I'm feeling very confused. Chris, an apprentice from several years ago, arrives, broken, sobbing. Bill was like a father to him and he is devastated. Will, another apprentice, comes to help with the shoveling. Tom, Riley, Sheila, Seppy, everyone gathers, and last of all, Jeff, with the simple wooden box, so lovingly crafted all throughout the night, made just for Bill's "remains." I love the word "remains" because the already decaying body is really all that remains of Bill.

Lots of things happen today. Leila ties my indigo blue scarf around Bill's head to hold his chin up. It makes him look adorable and I chuckle inside just a little bit. Wendy removes his tracheostomy tube and his stomach tube. I don't see that happen and I'm not sure I'd want to watch.

And when we call for women to wash him, there are eight volunteers including me. Sara, Leila, Wendy, Becky, Lisa, granddaughter Ruby, and Sheila surround the bed. Leila tears a towel into eight pieces and prepares a bowl of lavender-scented warm water.

I am at his right side and wash his shoulder, his arm, and down to his hand. I dip the cloth again and wipe his palm and between his fingers. His hands are covered with callouses from the hard work he did. Some of his fingertips are split from the winter's cold. His skin is cooling and becoming mottled in places, fading his freckles. I don't feel Bill is in his body anymore but that body served him well. He was an athlete in high school and college, he played tennis, he could outwork any twenty-year-old, and now his remains are already beginning to break down. He had the body of a man half his age. And he was a great roll in the hay.

As we go over his body with warm scented cloths, Sara says, "Dad, this is a dream come true. Eight women with their sixteen hands all over you." We all laugh. It's so true. He would have loved it.

We turn him to wash his back and I am shocked. His ass was always a perfect bum, smooth and round but it seems to be gone. "His bottom is deflated," I say. I'm serious but it elicits some great chuckles. Then I wonder to myself if all asses deflate at death.

When I suggest we wrap him in some kind of shroud for burial there is an uproar. Well, perhaps that's too strong a word. But there is some protest. Bill needs to wear what he always wears. I get some clean underwear from our room. We dress him in his accident jeans, tee shirt, flannel shirt. We're not going to bury him in his knitted vest. That's for me to keep. Leila takes charge and knows just how to put a shirt on a dead person who is going into rigor mortis. We all look aghast at how she's handling his dressing. And then someone remembers that she worked in a funeral home.

"He needs socks," someone says. My first thought is why would he need socks? But socks it is. And then his heavy work boots.

"There's something missing," someone says. "His glasses. He always wore his glasses."

I find the glasses that Tom and Riley had gotten made for him when his old ones went missing. My guess is the old ones are still guarding the secret of the accident. Someone puts them on, and he looks like Bill again. Now all he needs is his hat. It's blue with a "B" for Buppa sewed with beads at the crown that granddaughter Brianna made for him a few years ago. It's always been his favorite.

Becky makes sure I get into my office to make plans because she knows I need to. I write the obituary.

> "Farmer" Bill Thayer died at home early in the
> morning of April 1 at Darthia Farm, Gouldsboro,
> surrounded by loving friends and family. He got
> up at 4 a.m. every day, put in a full day's physical
> work, fell asleep every night after supper, sitting in
> his chair. He made the farm and the community
> a better place. When he had his accident, he was
> doing what he loved most, working his horses, Andy
> and Star, and cutting wood in his woodlot.
>
> He was a good father, grandfather, great-
> grandfather, husband, and friend. He raised hell
> as a young man in Boston and then tried out the
> insurance business, which wasn't his passion in the
> least. He then went back to school and became a

special education teacher working with emotionally disturbed children. Forty-six years ago he married his child bride, Cynthia.

Farmer Bill and his family moved from Massachusetts to Maine in 1976 and with the help of many young apprentices and old mentors, carved out a vital organic farm where they raised vegetables, animals, and farmed with Bill's beloved horses. He loved his community, serving as a Gouldsboro selectman for many years. He loved playing the drums in his many bop jazz bands and worshipped in the church of Dizzy, Ella, Monk, and Coltrane.

When Bill was hospitalized for his injuries, his grandson, Eric, wrote the following, "He's the strongest man I've ever known. He is the best man I've ever known, and if I can be anything like him, I'll be happy." And our friend, Brendan, said, "I've been driving thinking of all the moments, the life scenes where Bill and Cindy have touched my life. They are full color. Candles, sheep skin rugs and the twinkle in Bill's eyes. I was just saying to Candace how Bill is timeless. How he could have existed in any age as a warm and steady presence. I keep saying to him, 'Hold on so you can say goodbye the way you want to.'" And he did.

Farmer Bill was helped in his gentle passing by his wife; his daughters, Sara and Amy; his son Tom and his wife Riley; his grandchildren, Leila, Brianna, Sinai, and Ruby; his great-grandchild, Lia; his sister-in-law Lisa and her partner Don; and loving friends, Liz, Shepsi, Wendy, Becky, Art, Sheila, and Seppy.

Bill was predeceased by his parents, Barbara and Carl, his granddaughter, Melissa, and his brother-in-law, Peter Underwood. Cherishing many memories of Bill are his wife, Cynthia, his children, Sara, Amy, Alison, Tom, and Robin, his grandchildren Eric, Leila, Sinai, Ellen, Ruby, Laura, Brianna, and Susie, and great-granddaughter, Angelia. Throughout his life he loved and nurtured many other youngsters. including, Ella, Maiah, Margaret Mae, Hannah Rose, Pepin, Celeste, Per, Brendan, Ryan, Harbor, Cedar, Chris, Josh, Jonsie, and many more. His Canadian family will miss him. Lisa, Don, Bob, Wen, Sarah, Amy, Jonathan, Charlie, Ali, Josh.

Darthia Farm will continue to give tours to schoolchildren and provide organic food to the community under the stewardship of Shepsi and Liz.

He was buried on his beloved farm next to his granddaughter, Melissa. A Celebration of his life will be held at Hammond Hall in Winter Harbor on Saturday, April 6, at 3 p.m.

I go over it many times and show it to anyone who wants to see it. We make sure the hall is free for Saturday, April 6, all day. Becky will officiate. Everyone wants to be part of the ceremony. I get an email from my chorus director, Anna, who asks if I would like the chorus to sing at the service. Fantastic! And what would I like them to sing?

"'The Parting Glass'," I say, "We sang it several years ago, it's not complicated, and it's very appropriate."

Anna asks if I want to sing with them.

I tell her, "Sure." She will have a rehearsal with any chorus members who can make it. "I won't be able to rehearse or warm up," I say.

I put something on Facebook and more food arrives. Bill's "remains" hold court in the drum room. He looks very debonair, albeit a farming kind of debonair. The scarf is gone from his head. It's done its job. He lies in state with his hat, glasses, farm clothes, and big winter work boots. He's ready. For the first time, I realize Kelpie, our Nova Scotia Duck Tolling Retriever, who is really Bill's dog, has taken up residence in Bill's chair near the bed. She watches over him as people go by, touch his hand, say a quiet word. His skin is becoming more mottled but we are waiting for the paperwork for the death certificate to come through before we proceed. Wendy makes calls, tries to expedite everything.

About twenty-five friends and family are gathered for the vigil, waiting to go down to the cemetery. Some have come to help shovel. Some have never left. Lisa has been a quiet help, making food, answering the phone, greeting people. Her partner, Don, is the "go to" man regarding the site at the cemetery. Amy has arrived back from Portland. Still no sign of Alison or her children. Amy says there was no mention of Bill during the drive with Alison to Bangor. I can't imagine driving all that way and not bringing up the subject, but I'm sure Amy was afraid to make Alison angry. The beautiful wooden box, made by Jeff with love, waits just outside the door in the driveway. Someone passes out more food.

The wind has picked up, which can make the horses skittish. Shepsi brings them into the barn and is putting on their harnesses. He's pulled the red wagon Bill made up close to the barn and some of the people are helping him. Becky asks Shepsi if he feels OK about driving the team. He's never driven the wagon with the team before. Andy and Star were always Bill's horses, although Shepsi used them occasionally to do garden work. Shepsi has become a very good horseman.

"Are you feeling comfortable about doing this?" Becky asks.

Every year we took a picture of the farm family for our mail-order business. This was the last one that included Bill. Shepsi and Liz will be taking over the farm.

"I'm certain I can do it and I want to. I know I can do it," Shepsi says.

When Becky tells me how Shepsi responds to her, I know, too, that he can do it. It's a poignant moment of passing the reins, literally, from Bill to Shepsi. Bill would have found it almost impossible to watch it unfold if he were only able to watch from the porch, unable to participate, but this kind of "passing the reins," is what we've worked so hard to make happen so the farm would continue. Bill would be pleased to see Shepsi so confident and skilled, taking the reins from him.

Everything is in place. And we wait.

Chapter 30

PRESERVING THE FARM

Years ago Bill and I discussed ways to preserve our land for future generations. We contacted The Frenchman Bay Conservancy and put together an easement that would keep the farm and its thirty-five acres of land intact, prevent further building on the property, and leave border areas forested. We felt we had done a smart thing for the farm and for anyone who might own it after we died.

As time went on, we realized we needed more help than just seasonal apprentices, as the farm grew and our farm store got busier. We had branched out to include a busy mail order business, were selling to some restaurants, and took part in a farmers' market in Winter Harbor. We began to look for someone we could give some of the responsibility to and had several young farmers in that role. Dan, Jeff, Sonja, Lily, and Ivelisse. They were all great people but one wanted her own farm, one didn't like managing apprentices, one wanted to do something else other than the hard work of farming, and one had a new love interest.

Ivelisse stayed for four years and we adored her. She was happy here but she went back to Puerto Rico in the winters to help out her family who had health issues. We discussed having her take over the farm when we could no longer do it but it was an emotional subject. Our son Tom wanted the farm but didn't really have an interest in farming. He had built a beautiful post-and-beam house on the property, but he was a fisherman not a farmer.

Ivelisse, in a tearful admission, told us she was going to leave. The main reason seemed to be her family but she couldn't see herself being the main farmer on our busy farm. We were devastated to lose her since we had grown very close. We advertised with Maine Farmland Trust stating that we were looking for someone to take over running the gardens and eventually inherit the farm. We were in our seventies and although we were still very involved, we were aging and wanted to see the farm continue.

A family from New Mexico, a couple and their eight-year-old child, answered the notice in Maine Farmland Trust and, after many Skype calls, we decided we'd like to have them come. They sold their house and most of their belongings and arrived in an old car with everything they still owned. We were elated that someone was going to take over and allow us to slow down a bit and that they were so interested in continuing the farming operation.

It didn't take long to realize there was trouble in paradise. She had drinking problem. The second night they were here, she drank so much at an apprentice gathering she threw up all over the place. The child had some serious mental-health issues and the parents weren't watching her. She ended up in our house, going through our things. But the worst was Dom, the husband. We had two lovely apprentices at the time who worked hard and were kind and generous. Dom began to boss the young woman around. We didn't know how bad it was until she came to us in tears saying he was threatening her, shaking his finger at her, yelling, and being abusive.

Bill called a meeting for the next morning out on the patio behind the house, and addressed the problem with Dom. It didn't go well. Dom refused to even discuss the issue. Our poor apprentice was quietly sobbing, struggling to deal with the way she'd been treated.

"I want you out of here tomorrow," Bill said firmly, without being loud or angry. The stillness in the air was stifling. No one spoke. We sat there for several minutes before they returned to the cottage they were staying in and we went back into our house. Several *very long* minutes. The next morning when we got up early, we could see them carrying their belongings out to their car. We stayed in the house, peering out the window, not wanting to rile him up. We were afraid of him, too.

The next time we looked out, they were gone and we never heard from them again. We heard they moved back to New Mexico after many aborted attempts at settling in other places. He was so scary and unpleasant and she had such a drinking problem that we couldn't imagine them having a positive situation anywhere.

Our young apprentices stepped up and worked harder, but we really needed someone to take responsibility and be able to take over. We were tired of not being able to make it work. We were almost ready to quit, sell the animals, take down the sign, when a few days after Dom and his family left, we received an email from a young couple who was interested. They came to visit and we knew we had found someone who would love and nurture Darthia Farm like we did.

Shepsi, his long blond dreadlocks hanging down his back, was the dad of two towheaded children, Harbor and Cedar, who was still just a baby. Liz was tall and thin with a warmth to her that I loved. We had lunch, talked, and decided to meet again. After several meetings and a lot of thought, we all agreed. They'd like to be Darthia Farm's next stewards. Tom had bought another house on the next peninsula and moved out, so his house had become available.

Shepsi, Liz, and their small family moved into Tom's house down toward the bay and we began our journey. We set up an LLC with a lawyer giving them each two and half percent each per year up to a combined fifty percent so that they would immediately become part owners. None of our children or grandchildren had any interest in running a farm and Bill was especially passionate about doing everything we could to make sure Darthia Farm remained a working farm after we had poured all our money, time, energy, and hard work into bringing it back. Our children agreed.

We paid Shepsi a small salary so that he wouldn't have to work outside the farm. It was really a stipend but their food bill was minimal, their electricity was solar, and they heated with wood cut from across the street in our woodlot.

We grew fond of the family who were so thoughtful and kind. Shepsi took over working Archie, the third Haflinger. Liz made the best sourdough bread in the world. The children, aged one and four, were delightful and actually became a huge help with all the farm chores. Things were being done differently and sometimes it was hard for us to change, but it was working and we were all thrilled. They had a farm and we had a promise that the farm would continue in some form after we retired or died.

Chapter 31

BURIED WITH BARBIE

Time is passing and the death certificate still has not come through. Wendy tries to reach the "powers that be" again. She says it's coming along. There's no problem. It just takes time. But we don't have time. It's going to be getting dark soon and everything is ready. People are gathered, Bill is all set, the horses are getting their harnesses on, the wooden box waits just outside the kitchen door. Someone makes the decision. We're going to do it, death certificate or no death certificate. Wendy assures us that it is on the way.

The coffin won't fit in the door. They try both doors. No luck. It's way too big to fit. It's a comic moment reminiscent of bringing him home in the ambulance. For a long moment there is no sound. Everyone is thinking. And everyone is thinking the same thing.

A group of friends lift Bill's now small remains from the bed and carry his stiffening body from his bed in the drum room, through our farm kitchen, past the wood stove, and out the door onto the porch to the box, waiting on the ground right off the porch. While they are holding him, someone says we need a cushion between Bill and the wood floor of the coffin. I run to get one of our sheepskins from the couch in the living room to lay his body on, and then we get very creative.

Everyone has an idea what Bill will need in the afterlife although we don't really believe in a religious afterlife. It's raucous. In goes the naked headless Barbie doll that he and the grandchildren used to play with, when—because of the non-PC high heels and waspish waist— their mother and I refused to participate in any Barbie play. Leila would call him on the phone for a Barbie appointment and there they'd be, Bill in his chair, Leila on his lap, playing Barbie. Leila snugs the battered Barbie next to his heart.

Years ago from somewhere now long forgotten, a little plastic toilet that made a loud flushing sound, came into our lives. Bill used it for our telephone message, "wait for the flush and let 'er rip." Children have always loved that toilet and lately, Cedar and Harbor have taken to flushing it. It's a very kid-like thing and Bill was great with all of that. He had the skill of getting down to kids' level without being at all condescending. In goes the plastic toilet.

Someone puts a drumstick in each of Bill's hands and they stand right up as if he's getting ready for some fanfare. I lay his favorite picture of Dizzy Gillespie on his chest. Dizzy and Ella Fitzgerald were Bill's idols. He used to say that when he went to heaven, Dizzy would be there to greet him and trade some fours. And now he will be.

It's not like we believe he will need these things in the afterlife. Most of us believe in the love of community and nature rather than an old man in white robes. It's just because we need the ceremony of it all. Each year, when we go to Carriacou, I buy a few yards of material from our landlady's store with Grenadian colors to use to make a tablecloth. I haven't made one yet from our winter's trip so I unfurl the yards of new fabric and we drape it over him. The whole thing is so silly but sweet and tender at the same time. I picture him under the red, yellow, and green plaid cotton cloth, with his new glasses on, snuggling with Barbie, and holding his drumsticks, ready to play some cool bop.

I guess we're ready for the next bit. It seems so final too, but I know it's just one leg of the process of losing my husband, becoming a widow. It seems unimaginable. But I'm swept up in the momentum of it all and can't get off the train.

Jeff places the wooden top on the box and secures it. He's put ropes around it and friends and family pick up the box by the rope handles and carry it out to the waiting red wagon. Shepsi has Star and Andy all harnessed, hitched to the wagon, and ready to go. The pallbearers slide the coffin into the back of the wagon. Star and Andy, reins already passed to Shepsi, begin the short walk down to the Darthia Farm Cemetery.

Chapter 32

OUR SENSE OF PLACE

Place has always been significant in my life as a girl, as a woman, and as a writer. As a child I spent hours on Nova Scotia beaches, allowing sand to flow through my fingers, watching for a meandering crab that mistakes me for a stone or perhaps a dolphin who leaps in the nearby waters just for my enjoyment. As I grew, I lived in other places, but it was to the ocean that I was perpetually drawn. It seemed I could breathe deeper, stand up straighter, be more hungry, taste salt in my mouth. Bill shares that love of the sea and that's one reason our move to Maine was such a brilliant change for us. He grew up near the ocean, too, sailed as a young-ster, and loved to be in the water.

When we moved to Maine, we knew we had to live near the ocean in order to be happy. I wasn't sure whether it was the sound of surging seawater, the feel of beach stone under my feet, or the smell of rotting seaweed. I think for Bill it was the power of the ocean and the love of people who opt to live near the sea. But when we saw an ad in *Yankee* magazine that said, "old farm-house and barn, pink granite shore," I lobbied hard for my place by the ocean because it was more money than we had budgeted.

We drove up and shook our heads over the foot of water in the basement, at the layers of swallow and bat guano layering every surface of the old barn, at the scrubby alders covering every possible garden space. But when we walked down a quiet dirt road toward the shorefront that opened to a sand beach surrounded by rose-colored rock and lined with old apple trees, I breathed deep in that old childlike way. I crouched by a heap of rockweed and scooped up sand, let it dribble onto my foot.

Although the ocean was only a five-minute walk from the house, we didn't go down as often as I would have liked because our labor was so intense in those early farming days. But I knew it was there, and sometimes just the thought of putting my face into the saltwater and tasting the ocean was enough to get me through a stressful moment.

When I started writing fiction in 1996, I had an office in the house that was mine alone, that no one would enter without permission. Great, I thought. I have a room of my own. But as the farm grew busier and I grew older and less focused, I found it hard to ignore a distant phone ringing or the stack of bills on the edge of the desk, or a book, its corners turned down, begging to be finished. Bill supported me in everything I ever did and this was no exception. I needed somewhere else to write.

Virginia Woolf's quote from her famous essay came to mind, "Women, then, have not had a dog's chance of writing poetry. That is why I have laid so much stress on money and a room of one's own."

We didn't have much money, but we were comfortable and I had a room of my own, so what was the problem? I knew I had to have a separate room of my own. There were "rooms of one's own," and there were "rooms of one's own," and they were not all the same; additional distance was required. Bill understood completely and helped throw around ideas. The idea of a yurt at the ocean came to me as an epiphany one day while I was digging around in the sand. It was a perfect answer.

I contacted Borealis Yurts in Southern Maine and received one of their last units—a ten-foot-diameter simple yurt. I wasn't able to be at there for the delivery. We had a crew. "Please," I said to Bill. "Make sure the windows face the ocean. I had the windows put in especially to face the ocean."

I arrived at the site just a few feet from the water's edge about noon. I had a lightness to my step that I still remember. I was going to have my own writing house smack dab on our beloved ocean. As I rounded the last corner, I saw the windows, facing the path. "Bill. The windows. They're facing the woods."

"It's too late," he said.

The helpers all looked up, holding their hammers and tape measures. How could I not love them for doing their best. For putting up a yurt just for me.

"It'll be fine," I said.

It was a perfect mistake that Bill unconsciously made. The next day I walked into my yurt with my laptop and sat at the desk. The windows looked out at close woods. Not terribly interesting. Just scrub alder and dying birch. But I sat down and entered the world of my story without any distractions like ringing phones, or books to read, or a view of the ocean. I realize now that I needed to have the roundness of the yurt—no corners to hide in, no bills or books or anything that doesn't pertain to my writing, and a view that is of very little interest so that my mind stayed on my work.

A few years ago, an apprentice asked if she could do yoga in my yurt in the early morning, before I would be writing in there. I uttered an emphatic "No," and tried to explain that it was a writing place, not a yoga place. I'm sure she didn't really understand and perhaps thought me to be selfish. But the rule stood. No one may enter the yurt except for me and my dog and of course, Bill, if he asked nicely.

I wrote my novels in the yurt, summer and winter. No one dared come in and bother me in "a room of one's own."

My dog became used to the rhythm. Fifty minutes of writing. Ten minutes of breathing the ocean and throwing balls into the froth. Fifty minutes of writing. Ten minutes of rowing back and forth. Fifty minutes of thinking hard. Ten minutes of sifting sand through my fingers onto the surface of a granite boulder.

The ocean, to me, is freedom. Freedom to write what I want and live the life I want to live. It is a sign of the strength, love, ferocity, danger, and vitality of an untamable entity, right in my back yard. And the best part is that Bill understood perfectly and helped buy and set up the yurt—even knowing, subconsciously, that my idea about the windows wasn't quite going to work. Like Bill's dream of seeing Dizzy at the pearly gates, I want an ocean, strong yet nurturing, to greet me up there.

Chapter 33

FINAL RESTING PLACE

We follow behind the wagon, more than twenty of us, walking slowly the hundred yards or so down the farm lane to the small cemetery. It's April 1, April Fools Day, and snow still piles up in places. We pass our barn, the farm store, the little BnB from which my deathwatch bed was taken, past the dormant gardens and two of our large hoop houses. Star and Andy walk together as if they'd always been driven by Shepsi, looking like somehow they know they have a new teamster and Bill would want them to be on their best behavior. When we approach the little cemetery near Shepsi and Liz's house, Shepsi turns them and backs them up toward the hole that Jason dug until it's as close as he can get it. "Gee, Haw, Back," soft like Bill used to. It's not an easy job but they do it perfectly.

The box isn't very heavy. Bill lost a lot of weight in the ICU and the headless Barbie and the plastic toilet don't weigh very much, but the terrain is uneven. They walk the box up to the hole and set it on the ground. Shepsi stays with the team. The pallbearers position themselves on either side of the hole and lower the box until it rests on the bedrock and everyone gathers around. No one moves or speaks for what seems a long time. There's been no plan. Someone begins to sing a call-and-response song and others follow suit in beautiful harmony. Finally, after several verses, I pick up a handful of dirt from the pile and toss it into the hole on top of the wooden box.

"He needs some horse poop," I say. Someone brings a shovel full fresh from Star and throws it onto the top of the coffin. Disrespectful? Not in the least. Bill loved his horses and loved the smell of horse poop. It was totally appropriate. Others throw clumps of dirt. Leila digs into the dirt pile with a fury, using her bare hands. It's cold and the earth still is full of ice crystals. I try to get Leila to wear gloves. Chris collapses onto the ground in tears. Tom grabs a shovel and works in harmony with his ex-wife's husband, Seppy, filling the hole. The one thing that draws us all together is the love and admiration we have for Farmer Bill. We each have our own reasons for such strong feelings.

Although the hole is not deep, it is wide, which means it takes a lot of soil to fill it up, even with the box in there. Everyone helps. Some with shovels, others with bare hands. Leila still has not put on gloves. When the hole is filled we slowly file back to the farmhouse and crowd into the toasty kitchen. Someone has filled the woodstove. Evening is coming. The sun is going down. My sister and the others start passing out food and wine. The death certificate finally arrives, as we knew it would.

And when the house is full to overflowing and Bill's remains have been well buried, there's a commanding knock at the door. No one ever knocks here so it's startling. Most folks just come right in and holler. It's Tyler, Gouldsboro's chief of police, in full uniform. Bill, as a selectman, was technically his boss. I think to myself that it's a nice gesture for Tyler to come to pay his respects.

Someone lets him in and he tells me he wants to talk. I say that I have a full house of people and it isn't a good time.

"Please step outside," he says. "It's important." People are milling around, eating, talking but all that stops when Tyler speaks.

"I'll be right out," I say.

When we get onto the porch and close the door, I start to sweat. It's not to pay his respects. I know why. I can tell from his attitude. We didn't have the death certificate. But we do now. So, we're OK. He doesn't say he's sorry that Bill died, or he's sorry to barge in like this.

"Do you have permission to bury?"

"We have a cemetery. Right here," I say. "Just down the lane."

"What about a death certificate?"

I don't answer, pretend that I'm ignorant of any of that, pretend I'm too bereft to even understand what he's talking about.

He continues to press me. Suddenly, Leila comes out of the house.

"Hey Tyler, what's happening?"

From the conversation, I realize that they went to high school together. In an intimidation contest, Leila would win, hands down. She does. She asks what he's doing there. He backs down. Finally he leaves us alone and I go back inside, quite shaken and grateful that the death certificate did finally come through, albeit a little late.

The rest of the day and the days that follow are full of people, many Nova Scotia relatives, some neighbors, some bringing food, some relatives who are staying here. Our dear friend Colleen brings seafood chowder for everyone from The Pickled Wrinkle, our local pub and our best lettuce customer; another night she brings a pork tenderloin with everything to go with it, while we make plans for the service on Saturday. I send in the obituary to both the *Ellsworth American* and the *Bangor Daily News*. It costs a fortune. But that's the only expense there is and the cost was covered by the donations at the coffeehouse jazz night. No funeral home, no cemetery fee, no casket cost, no embalming cost, no frilly pink satin lining, no hearse. Not one penny has been spent by us to usher Bill on his way. And never have I been so touched by our caring community.

And all this time, life on the farm goes on. In the barn we have new lambs, which need watching. Community Supported Agriculture shareholders are putting in their orders. Horses, cattle, sheep, and poultry need to be fed, manure shoveled, eggs gathered.

Sheila says she'll take care of the music for Saturday. There must be music. We plan the rest. And every once in a while, I chuckle to think of Bill underneath the Carriacou plaid table-cloth-to-be wearing his glasses, hugging headless Barbie, poised to trade some fours with Dizzy and Monk.

Chapter 34

SUMMER CHICKEN

"Is it time for summer chicken yet?"

In most households, summer chicken could be any time, but at Darthia Farm, where all the ingredients, except for flour in the sauce, were raised on the farm, we waited until the basil was big enough to pick and we had enough vegetables growing in the garden for a proper presentation. Often we had to wait until the first batch of chickens had become large enough to slaughter unless we had some left over from the previous summer. We didn't usually eat this dish the day we slaughtered the chickens because chicken always tastes better if we wait at least a day and we are usually all too sick of talking, looking at, and working with chicken to want to eat it. For many of our young farm apprentices, killing and preparing chickens for the freezer was their first experience in this area. "Remember, tomorrow we have summer chicken," often kept them going because they had heard rumors about how good it was and needed to make some sense out of an often-difficult learning experience.

I sat down in the too-narrow row beside the basil bed, my ample bottom plopped on the very edge, bruising tiny leaves to release basil into the air. It's hard to keep picking the top leaves into the bucket, and not let myself fall face down into the center of the basil bed and roll down the entire length, the smell is so fragrant. The rest were watching. "Oh, is that how you do it?"

"When the bed is bigger, I use scissors, but for the baby basil, the basil for the summer chicken, only fingers."

No one but me was allowed to pick the first basil. They watched for a week. "Is it time yet?" they asked, anxious to learn how to make pesto. Soon the small bucket, the size of a chicken cavity, was full, and we moved to the next garden.

The carrots, as usual, were planted too close together, and I felt around on the top of the soil amongst the tops for thinners, which pulled out hard because the soil was dry. Tiny Rose Finn and Austrian crescent potatoes bounced into the empty pail, just a few. If we hadn't been using them for the summer chicken, we would probably have waited another week. These were the first of the season, too small to sell, but the best potatoes of the year.

The peas were picked, shelled, and waiting in the kitchen but it was too early for green beans and squash so we made do with the root veggies. On the way back to the house, I hesitated by the leek trench. Two bunches. That's all I needed. I felt a little guilty. If anyone else had pulled leeks this small I would not be pleased. But I could do it. Bill and I owned the place. I glanced down the path and saw that they were all busy weeding as I reached down and grabbed two bunches of tiny white leeks and placed them in the potato bucket. At the back door, I stooped to pick a big bunch of parsley and the last two peonies for the table.

"Wasn't it worth the wait?" I asked. We all gathered around the table for the promised dinner—Bill, my son, daughter-in-law, granddaughter, three apprentices—but they are too busy eating to answer. The idea that all the food was raised right here on the farm might just be too much for them to handle right now. So I wait until we have finished.

"I can't believe we grew all this," Kate says before I have a chance to remind them. "Every last thing."

"Except the flour," I said, glad I had waited.

"Next year we are growing wheat," Bill says.

I look around at the astonished faces of the young apprentices, realizing that they have acquired the knowledge that they can feed themselves and it frees them, just a little, from the bounds that modern society has placed on them.

Chapter 35

BILL'S BIG PARTY

The rest of the week is full of relatives and friends arriving, people calling for details, reading the hundreds of comments on email and Facebook, cutting out the many newspaper articles about him, taking the death bed to the transfer station and putting my bed back in the BnB cottage, reading myriad cards from folks who knew Bill, some still saying "get well soon."

My brother, Bob, and his wife, Wen, fly in from Toronto and check in at Elsa's Inn down by the harbor. The inn only charges half for their room. Our nephew, Jonathan, drives down from Nova Scotia and wants to stay in the A-Frame cottage. Lisa's children, Josh and Ali, arrive with their families and will stay in our BnB cottage. Tom Duprey, our trumpet player friend, and his wife Susan will stay with Shepsi and Liz. Somehow we house everyone else.

Leila contacts Pine Tree Services, which provides American Sign Language interpretation to make sure we can have an interpreter for Robin, who is being driven up from west of Portland by her caregiver for the service. Colleen brings more food because we have twenty or so people to feed every night. We work on the plan for the service. There could be a lot of people there. We send out the word to bring finger food. Becky, who wants to officiate at the service, goes to town for a few cases of wine, which are still being paid for by the coffeehouse donations.

The day of "Farmer Bill's Party" comes and we hustle to get dressed, make sandwiches, print programs, feed the hoards some breakfast, hope we have enough food and drink and plates and cups. We're all gathered in the kitchen when the call comes from Leila that she's on her way to Bangor because Robin's caregiver's car has broken down and they need to be picked up. They are an hour and a half away. That means both Leila and Robin, two of his most important people, will miss the service. Susan suggests getting them an Uber. We call Leila, then Uber. There are no cars. We call Lyft. Bingo. They're on their way to Bangor to get Robin and her caregiver. We tell Leila to turn around and go directly to the hall. We're ready. We pile into cars and head down to Winter Harbor.

In Prospect Harbor, a village of Gouldsboro where the town selectmen meet, we see the big electric sign at the local church, "Bean supper cancelled. RIP Bill Thayer." Just past the church, the flags at the fire station and town office are all at half-mast. As we get into Winter Harbor, the flags there are all at half-mast. It's as if the king has died.

The hall is all set up and my friends Cathy and Colleen are working the kitchen. My friend Nuna has ordered a massive amount of sushi, which has been delivered. The tables are covered with sandwiches, cookies, cakes, cheese, and crackers. Bill's daughters put together a slide show with myriad photos of the very photogenic Farmer Bill, which plays over and over along with some hot be-bop jazz that Sheila picked out. We find chairs in the front and mingle as people arrive. Becky has set up her podium. Alison's daughter, Susie, comes in, but doesn't speak to me. At least someone from that family came. Bill's entire jazz band is setting up on the stage and members of my chorus of

about twenty singers are mingling. I sit down close to the front
next to my sister and wait.

Leila arrives. Robin and her caregiver pull up in a Lyft car,
a bit shaken. And Pine Tree has sent two ASL interpreters for
Robin. One interprets the actual language and the other is deaf
and interprets the words from the first interpreter and repeats
it for Robin with the emotional part added in. Apparently they
often do this for deaths where it might be difficult for the deaf
person. They are amazing.

Our grandson, Eric, has brought his girlfriend whom we only
met briefly the previous fall. She's quite different from women
around here. She wears makeup and has her hair and nails done.
She seems sweet and I wish we could have met under different
circumstances. Sara's ex-husband is here with his new wife.
He's pretty emotional. He loved Bill. I don't turn around but I
can hear people coming in. It sounds like more people than we
imagined. Then the slides stop and the jazz band tunes up; all
professionals and all totally into playing in honor of their friend,
Drummer Bill. This time they were able to get Mike Bennett,
who is easily the best jazz drummer in the state of Maine and who
has given Bill several drum lessons over the years. They play a few
bop standards. Dizzy. Coltrane.

And then everything hushes. Mike Bennett begins his drum
solo. He's Bill. I can feel him through Mike's music. And then
the heartbeat begins. It builds and builds. Mike frantically throws
his hat on the ground. No one moves. He's channeling Bill all the
way. Then he moves into a heartbeat that slows and slows until
I can barely stand it. It slows and slows and finally stops. Mike is
exhausted. When he finishes there is silence for a long moment
and then applause.

Becky calls for the family to come up. I thought it would be
a good way to introduce everyone. It goes down the line: Leila,
granddaughter; Brianna, granddaughter; Jonathan, nephew;

Ruby, granddaughter; Sara, daughter; Susie, granddaughter; Sinai, granddaughter; Ali, niece, Zan, nephew-in-law; Eric, grandson, Lisa, sister-in-law, Josh, nephew, Isabella, great-niece, Amy, daughter, Rich, son-in-law, Don, brother-in-law, Bob, brother-in-law, Wen, sister-in-law; Robin, daughter . . . I say a few halted words of welcome and thanks and Becky introduces Shepsi.

Shepsi goes up to the stage, takes out his guitar, and sings one of the most touching, funny, and irreverent songs I have ever heard. (See the appendix.)

Brendan, Becky's son, tells the story of how Bill brought him into their cabin when he was just a day old, traveling by horse and sleigh because a snowstorm had prevented a truck from getting through. The chorus I've been a part of for twenty years sings a beautiful rendition of "The Parting Glass" in four-part harmony. I even sing with them, well, sort of. A word here and there. My brother speaks about his part in getting Bill and me together—lots of laughs. Hannah, Wendy's daughter, and Pepin, sing the call-and-response song, "The Farthest Field," that people sang at the grave, with everyone joining in.

Bill's dear friend, Dana, who is the head selectman in town and very stoic, emotionally speaks of his friendship with Bill. Robin, through the interpreter, signs a funny story about our early days. Our friend, Tom, the trumpet player, plays a piece for Bill, and then it opens to anyone who wanted to speak. Ex-apprentices, theatre and writer friends of mine, community members, all speak from the heart. And then Sheila puts on a CD of Louis Armstrong singing "What a Wonderful World." Everyone joins in and the sound swells throughout the hall.

I feel it is like the moment when everyone stands for the "Hallelujah Chorus." I can't stay in my chair. I stand and I hear those behind us rustling out of their seats, following suit. Halfway through the song, my sister says, "Turn around." She puts her arm around me and I turn. People are everywhere. Well over four hundred faces—upstairs in the balcony, crowding the lobby, on the main floor, are standing up are paying homage to Farmer Bill. I've never seen so many people in Hammond Hall. I smile at them, nod, and turn back to finish the song.

Chapter 36

THE SPINNERS' NAKED CALENDAR

I love to throw parties but not to be the center of one. When my 60th birthday was looming, Bill asked what kind of an extravaganza (his words) I was expecting. I knew inviting people and cooking for crowds was not his best skill and I also didn't want to be the center of attention so when the chance to do something wild presented itself, I jumped at it.

Our wool spinning group decided, while we were in a hot tub on a spinners' retreat, that we should look into doing a naked calendar like the women in England did. We could make some money and it would be a blast. Secretly, that could be my birthday celebration. When I mentioned it to Bill, his relief was apparent. I didn't want a party. I didn't want a big whoop-de-do. But I loved the idea of making a naked calendar with my spinning friends.

I was sure some people would he horrified but I didn't care. We were all excited about it, well, at least most of us. Bill has always loved my spinners. We still gather every Wednesday either at a hall or at someone's house, packing cookies and pickled beans and spinning wheels and bags of colored carded fleece to spin. When I had spinning here at the farm, Bill never strayed very far away from the house, mostly because of the great food, but he honestly enjoyed talking to the farmers, weavers, knitters, and shearers who gathered around the kitchen table at lunchtime.

Susanne originally came up with the idea of the calendar, replete with soup recipes, hints for choosing the perfect fleece, pictures of glorious socks and sweaters, and almost naked bodies wearing the socks and sweaters. We decided to donate a big chunk of the money to an environmental nonprofit and if there was anything left, we planned to use it to help fund our trip to Ireland.

Our first session began with a glass of merlot out in our hay-field and great hesitancy on the part of some. Most only needed a shout of "Everyone ready?" to begin a ceremonial tossing of all manner of clothing out of the camera's range amidst rollicking laughter. Our friend, Doug Trumbull, a photographer and film director, took photos of us walking hand in hand across a field, our assorted bottoms peeking out from beneath blue and purple and green colored patterns of handspun, handknit sweaters. My grandchildren wanted to be in the photo, too, so I gave them a couple of sweaters and they walked with us.

Another picture was of nine naked women, fanned out, prostrate on the grass, our glorious socks touching, our bare bums forming a dazzling array. One in our midst wanted to be in the photo but didn't want to disrobe. "Oh, please, join us, sure, wear your clothes," we said. Bill was sitting on the porch sipping his coffee, enjoying the beautiful day, when the UPS man drove up and did a double take at the scene. He smiled, shook his head a bit, and turned around after he left a package with Bill on the porch. His drive out was much slower than his drive in.

This whole thing was turning out way better than any party or celebration. I was turning 60, doing what I wanted to do, not what society expected. And, of course, Bill was having the time of his life.

We continued doing "shoots" of shearing sheep on a nearby island and slogging our spinning wheels through a mud rutted woods road down to our shore. We spun *en mass* at the edge of the sea from baskets of fleece, our wheels perched on rocks and seaweed strewn sand, our fingers silky smooth from the lanolin. Doug, the photographer, needed a "best boy" and of course, Bill volunteered. Bill held lights, passed Doug cameras, moved distracting flotsam out of the way.

We wore knee-high socks, one wore a magenta angora hat, we sat on sturdy rugs dyed with indigo and goldenrod from our gardens. We knit in a line on our porch from brightly dyed yarns. But the best was after we waited and waited for a snowfall, it finally came and we were ready for our December session.

Two of the younger spinners donned colored hats while Bill harnessed up the horses for their first sleigh ride of the season. I remembered that we had an old Santa hat in the closet so I grabbed it and tossed it to Bill as he went to unhook our Haflinger horses.

"Here, put this on," I said.

"Perfect." And he tossed his hunter's orange hat into the back of the sled and pulled the red and white one over his bald head. He looked like a Santa Claus with his white beard and sparkly eyes. Only thing missing was the big belly. The spinners scrambled onto the back of the sled and threw a blanket over their fronts so they wouldn't freeze and off they went. They circled around a few times so Doug could get a good shot, and each time they passed by us, Bill was looking back at the women, making sure they were comfortable. The final shot shows the sled from the back, two naked women sitting on a black sheepskin with Santa Claus ahead of them driving the horses, hat askew, and a definite twinkle in his eyes. The word traveled far that he was the happiest farmer in Maine that day.

My literary agent and her husband did the layout, which they sent to the printer. We were featured on CNN, *The Sun,* the *New York Daily News,* Fox News, even Japanese radio. We sold almost twenty thousand copies of the calendar and letters poured in from all over the world praising our courage and spirit.

Sure, it's easy to take off your clothes when you're young and confident with perfect skin and a size ten body. But when you're sixty or seventy or eighty and covered with sags and wrinkles and scars and rolls, it becomes easy when you're with people who cherish your ideas and your beauty, both inner and outer. Doug was one of those people. And so was Bill.

For me it was a time for wearing purples and greens together, for shaving my head if I wanted to, or for knitting a sweater that hung down to my knees. And I loved that I had a supportive husband who was having as much fun as I was.

Chapter 37

THE PARTY'S OVER

After Louis Armstrong's "What a Wonderful World," Colleen and Cathy put out the amazing array of finger food, including lobster and crab hors d'oeuvres, because that's what people do here. They fish for lobsters and there are usually crabs in the lobster traps. We put out our sandwiches made from lobster and hardboiled farm eggs. I'm not sure I've ever seen a more amazing array of finger food in my life. The huge platter of sushi has a long serpentine line of folks wanting to try it.

Sara's boyfriend, Duane, opens the wine that Becky bought with the coffeehouse donations. People mingle, cry, laugh. Our only regret is that we don't have the ex-apprentices stand up but then I realize that the hall is so crowded that half the people are standing anyway. The apprentices have come from all over Maine and other parts of New England. One flew in from New York City. There must be fifty of them here who worked under Bill as a mentor, many of whom now work their own organic farms.

On the way home we drive by all the flags at half-mast and the "RIP Bill Thayer" sign. People gather at the farm. Some go to the grave to see where he's buried. I can't do that. When I think about it, I begin to fall apart.

Eric, Bill's grandson, wants his sweater. It's a sweater Amy made for him years ago and he wore it often. Leila wants to bring his "slippers" back to New York. They're actually old work boots without laces that he always wore in the house and called his slippers.

I tell Mike Bennett, the drummer who played his heartbeat, that I'd like to give him Bill's drums for a student who can't afford a set. They're great drums and I'd love to have someone using them. I tell Mike that the cymbals were made for Buddy Rich. Bill's father knew Armand Zildjian pretty well. He was part of the Zildjian family legacy of making some of the finest drum cymbals in the world; the company can trace its roots back to 1618, when alchemist Avedas Zildjian, who was trying to change other medals into gold, discovered the perfect metal alloy for musical cymbals. Bill's father brought him to the Zildjian factory to pick out cymbals. Armand said to check out the three sets he made for Buddy Rich and choose one. Bill chose the best set.

I don't know how I'm going to live without him. The momentum is slowing down. I don't have any organizing to do anymore. As people leave for their homes, their jobs, their schools, I have a sense of panic. The first night I'm alone, I am fine. I wake up once, hearing someone call my name from downstairs. I don't answer. I know it's my mind playing tricks.

But the next day something really eerie happens. I take a nap in my office, which I rarely do, and as I'm waking up, I feel an arm under my shoulders and another under my knees, as if someone is picking me up. I don't open my eyes. But the arms stay for quite a long time and I allow them to hold me. Part of me, the atheist part, knows damn well it's my imagination, but I actually feel them and I know that it's Bill, or at least, the love that I have for him is creating the illusion of Bill and if there were in fact, a God, or an afterlife, Bill would want me to know that he thinks I'll be all right.

I tell Becky about this. She then calls every morning to see if I've had another visitation from Bill. I awaken a few more times in the night to my name being called but the sweet cradling never returns.

People don't want to leave me alone, afraid that I won't be able to cope, that I won't know how to light a fire in the kitchen woodstove, that I will fall downstairs, that Kelpie won't get any attention. I just work hard at creating a life without Bill. I feel that if I knew what happened there in the woods, I could move on with that knowledge. Liz and Shepsi went through the logging trails and saw wheel tracks on a telephone pole at the entrance that implied that the logging arch had tipped and hit the pole. But there were no glasses. If it happened there, his glasses would be on the ground. My guess is that something happened before the horses reached the pole at the entrance to our woodlot. By now, I'm back directing *Lost in Yonkers* and I ask Brent, one of my actors who seems to have everything, if he has a metal detector. He does, and brings it to the next rehearsal.

Becky comes with me as we wave the detector over the ground, searching for the glasses. The snow has mostly melted from the roads through the woods, so the terrain is different from when he had the accident. We walk where we figure he might have been, looking for anything suspicious—a fallen log, a big hole in the ground, a mangled culvert. We find old nails, bits of metal tools. We walk the entire circle of where he might have gone to bring logs back home. Because the snow is gone now, there are lots of holes in the ground made from frost. We wave and wave the detector over spots that might have been where it happened. He had forgotten the logging chain in the barn that day, so we watch for sled marks turning around. He would have noticed and come back to get it.

We talk about the woods and how quiet it is. We see tracks of coyotes and deer. We find nothing that shows a spot where he might have fallen or been hit by a tree, lost his glasses, and lost control of the horses. The metal detector beeps at everything but glasses.

Chapter 38

SLEIGH RIDE

One late February afternoon, Bill asked if I'd like to go for a sleigh ride. Usually I'm in the kitchen making cocoa and putting cookies on a platter for the folks who are on the sleigh ride so I don't often get to go.

"Sure, I'd love to," I said. "Can we put the sleigh bells on?"

"Sure, Dolly," he said. "I'll get them harnessed. It'll be a few minutes."

"I'll be out soon," I told him.

A few snowflakes were falling but not enough to amount to anything substantial. I pulled on my boots and tied a scarf around my neck, and threw the dog a couple of treats. "Behave yourself," I said. And off I went.

When there's a fresh layer of snow on the ground, sound changes. The crunch-crunch of yesterday's crust was gone, replaced by an almost noiseless hush. I walked toward the barn, kicked up soft snow, watched it swirl around before it settled again on the ground.

The bobsled that Bill put together waited at the corner of the barn entrance. Star and Andy were tied outside, all harnessed. But the sleigh bells weren't on. "Sleigh bells?"

"Oh. Forgot."

And he turned back into the barn. After our drastic fire when everything was lost, I bought him a set of refurbished antique sleigh bells for the horses, which sound just like what I imagined jingle bells sounded like when I was little. Red blankets lined the bed of the bobsled. I usually sat in the back but that day I felt like sitting up front next to him so I could see things the way he did.

"Oh, you're sitting up here with me?"

"Yep. I am."

Bill hitched the team to the bobsled, checked the chains to make sure they were even. Then he attached a set of sleigh bells to each horse, around their necks just behind their collars. Flurries continued to fall, adding to the soft snow on the ground. When the horses were ready, Bill untied them from the rope attached to the barn and hopped on the seat at the front, right next to me.

"Nice to have you up here with me," he said. "Git," he said softly to the horses.

I hardly heard him but the horses did. They began to pull the sled down the driveway toward the road. The only sound was the light jingle of the bells each time they stepped. We veered off the driveway to make our way across the hayfield toward the neighbor's driveway. The wind picked up and I wished I'd worn a hat. I pulled my scarf over my head to keep the wind from blowing in my ears.

When we got to the neighbor's driveway we turned left toward the road and our woodlot. He stopped them just at the edge of the road and got out with his shovel. By now, the plow had moved the snow and the salt truck had been through so the road was bare. Not the easiest terrain for sled runners. He shoveled snow over the macadam until it was deep and wide enough to accommodate the sled and climbed back on.

"Git," he said again.

He drove the team cautiously across the road and up into our woodlot. At the opening, two roads branched out in different directions and Bill took the one going to the left, à la Frost, the less traveled. The new snow stuck to the trunks of the pines, spruces, and firs. I felt his body next to mine, moving with each little adjustment to the reins. The horses walked slowly but I knew that, up ahead, Bill would let them trot.

The pine branches were laden with ravens, checking us out and cawing half-heartedly every once in a while. Nothing else moved there in the woods. Now that we were on the woods road, the wind had settled down to still crisp air. I took my scarf off my head and wrapped it around my neck.

"Here," he said. "Take the reins."

I loved driving the team but I didn't do it often. I realized I hadn't worn gloves, either, in my haste to get ready. But the air was mild and my hands felt fine for the moment. The flurries were sparse and I could see some blue in the sky. It was a perfect day.

Then I saw something on the snow ahead. A patch of red. I halted the horses.

"What's up?" Bill asked.

"Look. Up there. On the snow." I gave him the reins and slid down from the driver's seat onto the soft cushion of new snow and walked over to the splotch of red. As I drew closer, I saw the markings on the snow around it. "It's a fresh kill," I said. "Looks like a bird did it."

"Did what?"

"I'm looking." I searched around the small area, checked the blood spots until I found a rabbit tail. That's all. Just the tail surrounded by fresh blood. "I think it's a rabbit. But it's daytime. Owls and hawks hunt at night. Maybe it happened early this morning."

I tucked the rabbit tail into the pocket of my jacket and bent down to look at the marks in the snow. Definitely wing patterns. Something big. Great horned owl, or maybe a large hawk. I wished I'd brought my camera. The red against the white was striking and the patterns of the wings were so intense they would show up in a picture. I don't think he saw me pocket the rabbit tail. I was always bringing home bits and bones. I've had a petrified frog on the shelf in the kitchen for years and a donkey skull hangs on the wall of the living room. We didn't really need a rabbit tail.

I climbed back up on the sled. "You drive now," I said. I knew we were coming up to a sharp turn and he would probably have taken the reins anyway. Although I rode horses for years, I'm not terribly experienced in driving horses.

We turned the corner and Bill made a quiet kissing sound. The horses perked up and went into a lazy trot along the snow-covered road. The bells sounded louder, jingling with each trot. Some snow fell from a pine tree onto my head. When we turned again, Bill slowed the team to a walk as the sled bumped along behind us. The snow stopped and the sun came out. The snow on the ground sparkled. It was the most glorious scene I had seen since the last sleigh ride.

We didn't talk. We loved the quiet. Not even hooves plodding through the soft snow was audible. Just the jingle of sleigh bells and the occasional thump of the rear runners against a tree.

"I'd better take this shortcut. It'll be getting dark soon." Bill drove the team onto another road toward home. When we turned from the neighbor's driveway onto the pasture and back onto our driveway, I saw the moon rising just at the end of the drive. Again my thoughts turned to Robert Frost and I understood exactly what he meant about the road less traveled. We were taking that road.

Chapter 39

LIFE GOES ON

Cards continue to arrive and soon I have a huge basket overflowing with them. People pop in. The big question is "How are you doing?" I don't know how to answer that. If I say I'm just fine, they'll question my sanity and my love for Bill. If I say I'm totally fucked up, they won't know what to say and they'll hover. I am doing all right. I miss him terribly but I have no regrets about us as a couple. We loved each other, respected each other, never said a mean word although we occasionally disagreed. We never argued; we laughed a lot and loved to touch each other. I'm going to miss that the most, just touching him casually, leaning against him.

Directing the play keeps me busy. Perhaps that's good. We rehearse hard and the actors and tech crew give it everything. I work them until they are exhausted. It's an ensemble so I have them practice covering for each other, staying in character even if lions and tigers come into the hall. They are all amazing.

The first night's performance of the second weekend is going really well. Actors, including the boys, are totally that family in the stifling hot Yonkers apartment who are wearing uncomfortable clothes and dealing with challenging family dynamics. The noise begins toward the middle of the play. From behind where I sit at the sound board comes a strange grunting, which gets louder and more bizarre. It's a voice but no words, just sounds. Then it stops. And then it begins again. Most of the time it is quiet enough that the actors' lines can be heard over it. I notice that their voices become louder when the noise starts up again. Even the boys know how to handle it. It sounds vaguely like a wild animal but it must be a person with some kind of a problem. I glance over to where the sound comes from and see a young man with an older woman. It continues intermittently for the rest of the play.

I watch my actors. From them there's not a sign that anything is amiss. They all act right through it. Our hard work on being able to focus in spite of any odds is paying off. I find out after the play that a man was having a Tourette's episode.

And sometimes I feel like the actors—I just keep going. Gradually I allow myself a little alone time to feel the pain, in increments, just as much as I think I can handle. I still can't bring myself to walk the few steps down the lane, past the hoop houses and the horse training ring, past the strawberry plants, to Bill's grave. Each time I consider it, I well up with tears straining to flow out. I can't do it yet. But I often imagine what his body is like, glasses on, drumsticks in his hands, Barbie at his side, toy toilet on the other side, with his flesh slowly becoming dust. I give away most of his clothes, I plant succulents that Sara gave me for Christmas in the tops of his tall rubber boots, I comfort Kelpie when she howls at nothing. She still searches for him before the howls come.

Before the accident, Bill wanted to take me, Sara, and her wonderful new boyfriend to Paris the following fall. When he ended up in the ICU, I presumed Paris wasn't going to happen, but one day Sara called and said, "When are we going to Paris? Is it still on for this October?" So we are going. Sara, my friend Colleen, Sara's friend Joni, and me. Bill and I loved Paris. His favorite part of the trip was sitting outside the corner café in the

Colleen and me in Paris. The time I went to Paris before this, Bill and I went on this merry-go-round – me very willingly, he under duress.

evening, drinking wine, watching people go by. It was hard to get Bill to go to Bangor and impossible to get him to agree to a New York trip, but he was always ready to fly to Paris.

Sometimes I question taking him off life support in the hospital. Today, friends come to help get rid of some of Bill's town papers. We clean out his file drawer, throwing out years of now useless town government information. Underneath it all is a small bottle. I pick it up. Sleeping pills. And another. And still another. Six bottles altogether. I gather them up and put them in the bathroom, out of sight in the closet. This discovery is a turning point. Of course he wouldn't want to live unless he could be useful, active, and able to work his cherished horses. He was making sure he had the control to do something about it in case something happened. Something did happen, but I had the control.

In his advance directive, he named me to make decisions for him if he was unable to do so. We had often talked about the fact that we didn't want to live if we weren't living a good life. If we couldn't do the work that we loved and became a burden on someone else, that had to be the end. So I wasn't at all surprised to find the pills.

Bill was 82 years old, albeit a young 82, but he was getting forgetful. He seemed to have become smaller and had some leg problems when he worked. But he was living his life to the fullest. It wouldn't have worked to have him come home severely compromised, unable to work and play his drums and drive to Young's Store every morning to get his coffee and the *Bangor Daily News*.

I've always believed that some good comes out of all bad and I've been able to think about those things. Good that he isn't drooling on the porch. Good that I'm not suctioning phlegm for years from the throat of someone who doesn't know I'm doing it. Good that we had such a great ride for over forty-five years. Good that we were able to bring him to die on the farm he helped create out of an overgrown, neglected summer property. Good that he didn't get to the point of needing to use those pills, which probably wouldn't have worked anyway.

I'm practicing the walk down to the place where he's buried. Mixed feelings of comic hysteria about the things buried with him and the grieving hysteria that makes me think I can't bear going down there keep getting in the way. I either laugh or cry and I want to go when I can do the walk without laughing or crying. My friend Joe is going to carve his name on a stone bench so I can sit down there in the peace and quiet of the early morning farm.

Dear Becky is going to help me find some native plants that don't require lots of care to plant on the grave. I think I want to go down alone when no one is around. I'm a fierce and brave person in most circumstances, but this one scares me. I spend some time imagining the accident, what happened, how he felt, the amount of fear and pain he had, the relief he might have felt when I told him we'd take care of the horses.

But I'm still afraid to go to the grave.

Chapter 40

WHAT HAPPENED?

Becky and I never found the glasses that day in the woods.
I thought we would know what happened if we were to find his
somewhat grungy metal-rimmed glasses that must have flown off
his face during whatever happened to him. But now I'm not sure
it's so important. He had an accident, he struggled to come back,
and then he died. I've spent many hours trying to understand
how he ended up crumpled in a heap on the center line of Route
186 just outside the entrance to our woodlot and what he experienced during the accident. Here are some of my thoughts.

The horses walked slowly down the driveway toward the path
through the hayfield that would lead them to the woodlot across
the road. There was still some snow on the frozen ground, being
only mid-March. Shepsi told me later that Bill had forgotten the
chain for the logs. Bill sat on the tractor seat of the logging arch
as they pulled him across the meadow, the logging arch's wheels
lurching when they hit a large stone or a hummock. He loved to
work with the horses when the air was crisp and there was enough
snow on the ground to help the logs slide easily and avoid picking
up gravel along the way.

When they got to the road, he stopped so he could look both
ways carefully. Sometimes big trucks from the lobster cannery
in Prospect Harbor roared by without caution. When he saw

the way clear, he gripped the reins. "OK, boys." Star and Andy picked up the pace crossing the road and broke into a trot up the hill into the woodlot.

All versions of this tale begin this way. But then they vary.

Version One:

The two logs Bill needed to haul out were beside the woods road that swerved to the left. "Haw, boys. Haw. Easy." Star and Andy turned at his command and carefully walked down the center of the old woods road until they neared the two logs. He watched the sides of the road looking for holes that might be covered with snow so that the horses wouldn't slip into one and hurt themselves. When he passed the logs, he turned the horses and the arch and brought them alongside the logs. He jumped down and reached for the chain to wrap around the logs, attaching them to the back of the arch.

"Well, boys. I guess I forgot the chain. Back we go." He climbed back into his seat and took up the reins again. He stood up, although his wife had often cautioned him to stay in the seat. If he was going to get those logs hauled back to the farm before dark, he needed to move a little faster. "Git, boys." And Star and Andy began to trot along the snowy path. At a turn in the road, one of the wheels slipped into a hole, throwing him off balance and he fell off the arch, hitting his head on it.

He tried to say "whoa," but it wouldn't come out. Without their driver, the horses began to panic, which caused them to move faster. By the time they got to the entrance of the woodlot they were at a full gallop in their turn onto Route 186. He was still on the ground, his head feeling very strange. His glasses had flown off into the woods. The horses. He had to stop the horses. They would hurt themselves.

He heaved himself up so that he was standing. "Whoa," he said, but it was barely a whisper and by that time, the horses were halfway up Route 186 and galloping toward the main highway. He staggered along, catching himself on a tree branch and then on another. He slid down the little hill onto the road from the lot and heard the hooves pounding the macadam. "Whoa," he said again as he walked a few feet down the center line toward the sound. He tried "Whoa" one more time before he collapsed on the yellow line like a bag of rags, listening to the hooves clattering down the road toward the highway.

Version Two:

He drove the team straight ahead rather than taking the road to the left that he often did. He'll just pick up the logs on the way around. That way he won't have to turn them. He loved the woods when it was still and quiet. He stood up, holding the reins so that he could watch for holes along the side. The horses seemed a bit anxious. That was unusual. "Easy," he said. But the horses tossed their heads and put their ears back.

From out of nowhere, a deer bounded from the woods straight into the path of the horses. Behind the deer ran two coyotes, obviously after the deer. Bill tried to pull the horses to the side, slow them down, but Star and Andy reared up, jerking the logging arch, throwing him off onto a boulder.

The coyotes and the deer disappeared into the woods. Star and Andy reared again before they ran the entire circle and came out of the entrance at a full run, veered left, and headed for the highway.

He passed out when he hit his head on the boulder, his hat protecting his head from being cut. His glasses went flying into the woods, just at the spot that the deer entered. When he regained consciousness, he realized he was injured—but strangely enough there was no pain. He felt confused and forgot what he was doing there on the ground, the horses gone. He dragged himself back to the entrance to see if the horses were there. From a distance he could hear them galloping down Route 186, away from the farm, away from him. He followed as far as he could before collapsing at the center line. "The horses. The horses."

Version Three:

He realized as soon as he entered the woodlot that he had forgotten to bring the chain so he could wrap the logs and attach them to the logging arch to bring them back to the farm. "Whoa," he said just as the team got to the clearing. He stood up to turn them around, and stood up for better control in the small space. That's when he heard the tree next to him crack. He stopped the horses and stared up at the tree, which was coming down in slow motion toward him. In his haste to move the horses away from the tree, he fell from the logging arch just as the large main branch whacked his head. His glasses fell off and landed in a trench on the side. The branch settled. He was off to the side under the branch. The horses, frightened, raced out of the lot onto the road.

Bill knew he had to get out from under the branch so he pushed it off and staggered to his feet, hearing the pounding hooves of his horses running away. He fumbled for his glasses but couldn't find them. He had to get to the horses. They could get hit by a car. Anything could happen to them. He struggled toward the sound but when he reached a spot just a few feet down Route 186, he collapsed in the middle of the road. He just couldn't walk any longer.

"I'm afraid this is the end of the line," he mouthed just before he lost consciousness, there on the center line. "Please God, take care of my horses."

Maybe none of these versions is close to the one that happened. Perhaps it was something entirely different. But whatever it was, his glasses are there, in the woods, somewhere—hidden under a tree, at the bottom of a pool of water, crushed into the soil by a horse's hoof. And left in those woods was his essence. Somehow he separated from himself and could never join his body and his spirit back together, even though he tried with everything he had.

He struggled to save the horses from danger, he struggled to squeeze doctors' hands and to sit up at the side of his bed, he struggled to live until we got him home to his cozy farmhouse with the woodstove burning, his family and friends around him, and smells of good food drifting through the kitchen.

Although I don't and probably will never know what happened in those darkening woods that caused the severe head trauma that he experienced, I do know a few things. I know that he loved me and tried with all his being to come back to all of us. I know that he would not have wanted to live in a severely com-promised state. I know that he knew we were bringing him home to die at his cherished farm surrounded by people who loved him and knew how to sing if they wanted to.

I can only hope that he knew I'd be all right but that I would miss him terribly. I hope he knew that I'd be brave enough to try taking money out of the ATM, which he called the "money take out," and to go to Carriacou without him.

I'm sure he didn't know that I'd struggle with visiting his grave. I'm sure he didn't know that I'd meet a 118- year-old woman named Ms. Massima, who would change my thoughts on life and death. And I'm really sure he didn't know that on the anniversary of his accident, I planned to eat two red hot dogs, fried in our old cast iron pan, slathered in mustard and relish, served on a linen napkin.

Chapter 41

GOING TO THE GRAVE

Sara and I go to Paris in a few weeks and I'm going to tuck my memories of Bill inside my suitcase. This experience has made me understand that we all are born and we live for a while, sometimes a long while, sometimes very short, and then we all die. That seems obvious but I think that most of us don't really understand or believe it. I don't believe there's any grand design to any of it. It's mostly serendipity, destiny, luck, kismet. Anything can happen to any of us at any time. I'm probably next and that doesn't scare me nearly as much as it used to. I'm not sure Bill had any fear of his own death but it would have been hard for him if I had died first. That's another "good" to think about.

His cooking skills weren't great but he could probably live on stir fries, meatloaf, and red hot dogs. He knew how to cook a meal so he wouldn't starve. He'd never change the sheets, though. I told some friends that if I died first, to please remind him to change the sheets. And he'd be so lonely. I'm lonely, but I think I know how to cope with it better than he would have.

And stuff! I have so much stuff he would have to deal with. Fourteen spinning wheels, wool everywhere, a music doll someone gave me when I was six that turns around and around and has lost most of her hair, a freeze-dried frog that I found at the shore over forty years ago, a donkey skull I smuggled back from

Carriacou, boiled the flesh off, bleached, and hung in the living room, and twelve pairs of Crocs, all colors.

Bill had his drums and very basic clothing. His horse equipment is being used by Shepsi. Otherwise he didn't have very much. I guess you could say he was a minimalist. And I'm struggling to stay off that hoarding TV show.

In September, Becky calls and asks if this is a good day to go to Bill's grave to talk about plantings. It's been almost six months since his death and I still haven't been to his grave. Every time I think about going, I panic. But I tell Becky that it's a good day.

I'm prepared for the worst, whatever that might be. I could become hysterical, I could start to sob and not be able to stop. I could collapse and have to be hospitalized. Becky arrives in her truck with the back full of perennials, as well as seeds that won't require much watering or care. I'm kind of a wreck. It's been months of worrying about how to walk those steps down to where Bill is buried. But I walk with her, slowly, down past our farm store, past the little BnB, past the horse training ring, past the two big hoop houses that are in full production, past the old pine, and to the cemetery.

Becky knows how nervous I am and is kind and patient with me. I begin the short incline up to the bare mounded grave and feel fine about it. Becky sets down her box of seedlings and puts her hands on her hips. She's thinking about where to put the plants.

The cemetery needs work. Parts are overgrown and some of the big trees should be taken out. The scent of pine and of damp earth is everywhere. A few feet away is the granite bench inscribed with the word MELISSA across the top. In the summer, there are flowers here and there but today, late September, things look bare. The short rail fence we hurriedly erected when Melissa died to mark the boundaries of the cemetery is collapsing in spots and needs to be replaced. Several of the bars are rotten and have fallen out of the posts. The day is still. No one is about. The horses whinny now and then. Becky gets to work. She's brought enough plants to fill the mound, tucks one in firmly with her spade and moves on to the next. We have seeds, too, of flowers that don't require watering or a lot of pampering.

"How are you feeling?" she asks.

"I'm fine," I say. "No. Really. I'm fine. Just thinking of the Barbie and the toilet and the drumsticks and the horse shit."

We laugh together. I question why I was so nervous about coming here. And now I'm sure Bill isn't in that coffin at all. I knew that. I knew the man I loved with everything I had was gone and had been gone since that day something terrible happened in the woods. And my guess is that we'll never know what happened because we'll never find those glasses. Perhaps it's no longer important to know what happened in those woods.

I know that he was glad to come home. He knew that we all loved him and tried hard to bring him back to the old "Farmer Bill." I glance over to the mound, watch Becky so tenderly planting perennials that will bloom next summer and not need watering.

I imagine Bill, in his beautiful wooden box, hugging Barbie and saying, "wait for the flush and let 'er rip."

I kneel next to Becky, take one of the seedlings, place it in a hole, pat down the soil around it. We plant them all, cover the mounded grave with small green plants.

When we finish, I shrug. "What the fuck?"

Coda

GOING TO CARRIACOU

In May, two months after Bill's death, I made a decision. I was going to Carriacou for Christmas. I made the plane reservations and called to make sure the little apartment above Lucelle's store was available, right on the beach in the main town of Hillsborough, Carriacou, West Indies, where we had been coming for almost twenty-five years, usually with one or two grandchildren in tow. Bill's heart was on the farm but it was also on this small island far away, in the Windward Islands, the Grenadines, close to Venezuela. We have made many friends there and we both were able to step off the little six-seater at the airport and immediately relax and get into reading/swimming mode.

December comes. It's a big trip and I've aged years since Bill died eight months ago. It takes two days of travel and four flights to get there. I feel weaker, less alert, but I feel it's important to go. Most of all, I need the time and space to grieve, whatever that's going to mean. I need to be alone with my thoughts. The farm is always very busy with people coming and going and lots of work to do, and so, as my actors in *Lost in Yonkers* did when faced with a major distraction, I kept my focus, said my lines, inhabited my character. It was time to get away from the distraction and allow myself to be in a place Bill loved and find him there.

The little plane lands softly on the runway and Sunkey is waiting to pick me up. The small airport has about three other cars parked waiting to pick up someone. The balmy breeze hits my face and I know I am in a good place. Sunkey gives me a hug and carries my bag to his jeep, then throws it in the back. We chat about his dad, who died soon after Bill. He catches me up on the latest gossip and news on the island.

Along the short ride to Lucelle's, palm trees bend and sway and the waves crash on the sand right beside the road. We stop on the main street amid the hustle and bustle of Hillsborough, and Sunkey helps me with my one little bag. We climb the stairs to the apartment Bill and I have rented for many years after the "Resort" was abandoned; I know this year will be the same and different. The same because the ocean and the sand are still there. Same furniture, same view, same smells. But no Bill.

I've done the drill many times but never alone. It takes me just a few minutes to unpack because I always travel carry-on. The bags of spices go on the counter along with the disposable salt and pepper shakers. I love to cook and don't want to buy big containers of a spice like cumin or coriander that I might only use once or twice, so I put lots of different spices in sandwich baggies. I'm surprised I haven't been stopped by the drug-sniffing dogs at the airport.

I bring a bag of good coffee because it's not always available, as well as garlic from our garden because all the garlic on the island is from China and what's a curry without garlic? And the SteriPen water purifier. The water pitcher we bought a couple of years ago is still on the shelf so I purify some water with my UV magic wand and make some ice. Carriacou has little ground water, so water comes from a rainwater cistern, which contains bacteria foreigners aren't used to. Becky suggested I get the SteriPen, after I spent years buying water at the grocery.

The hardest things to unpack are the binoculars I gave Bill for Christmas years ago and the laminated sheet of flags of the world. We spent hours watching boats come and go and identifying them by their flags and names. I throw open the big doors to the balcony, move out a couple of chairs, and set up the binoculars.

"Look, Bill," I say aloud. "Got the binocs!"

After I get settled in and unpacked, I go out to town to get some supplies. Rum, nutmeg syrup, limes, pineapple juice, nutmegs, Angostura bitters, all for the rum punch, which is very important. Then I check out what the ladies on the street are selling. Tomatoes, avocados, grapefruit, bananas of all kinds, onions, oranges, callaloo, and dasheen, or taro. The sweet little bananas are perfect for bananas flambé, and the callaloo, which is the green part of the dasheen root and a little bit like spinach, makes the most amazing soup.

Then I walk down the street to Patti's Deli for some shrimp and basmati rice, greeting people I haven't seen since last year. I'm all set for Christmas Day and Boxing Day, when everything closes up tight. Christmas Eve is a real party time. Many of the Kayaks as well as the ex-pats stay up all night drinking rum, playing music, and dancing, so by Christmas morning they are sleeping or struggling to recuperate from the great time they had the night before.

I listen to the festivities from my balcony on Christmas Eve, sipping my rum punch, wondering if I will miss opening the stocking that Bill always put together for me, full of some of the same old things and always a couple of surprises that would make me laugh. Always a jar of artichoke hearts. A bar of good chocolate. Maybe a pair of socks. Always some kind of kitchen widget or gadget. Maybe an irreverent bumper sticker for my car. There would be no stocking tomorrow.

On Christmas Day, I read one of the many books I downloaded to my Kindle, based on friends' suggestions, and make myself a shrimp dinner for later to go with my Christmas rum punch. I never drink hard liquor other times of the year, but here, the sun and the waves whisper *rum punch*. A friend from Massachusetts who lives here half the year kindly invited me for Christmas dinner, but I declined because I really need to be alone. I know that friends and family back home worry that I'll be sad and lonely. Well, I will, but that's part of being a human being.

There's not a sound from town. Everyone's sleeping after a raucous Christmas Eve. Part of me is overjoyed to just sit and read instead of cooking and setting the table and opening presents. This year I couldn't imagine celebrating Christmas the way we usually do, with a great feast, a decorated Charlie Brown tree, lots of colorfully wrapped boxes, pine branches everywhere, Christmas crackers, roast beef and Yorkshire pudding, all without Bill. It's a good day. I read, think about everything that has happened. Sad? A little. Lonely? Perhaps. But no cooking. No dishes. No gathering up torn wrapping paper.

I sit on the balcony, overlooking the jade sea, and watch for boats coming in. A large schooner has moored right in front and I look through the binoculars to see what's happening out there. I think they're all sleeping, too. The palm tree right next to my place is loaded with coconuts and when a group of teenagers goes by and shakes it, some fall. The kids gather them up in a towel and continue their walk at the water's edge. It's rare that any people are on the beach and on this Christmas Day; the coconut shakers are the only ones I see. A few dogs go by.

Later in the afternoon, I swim my Christmas swim. The water is still and warm. I dive down, swim underwater, bob back up. And again. Some small fishes bump at my legs, each time making me jump. I stay in the water until my fingers are wrinkled. The sea has become a little rougher and getting out is a bit of a challenge but I make it on the second try.

I heat up the shrimp that I made earlier in the day, put together a salad with the avocado and tomato, mix up some callaloo soup, and prep the bananas for the flambé. An amazing meal, especially the bananas.

"Remember the flambé, Bill? Your favorite. I put a little extra rum in it just for you."

I tell Bill about the dogs on the beach and seeing Nellie on the street. I tell him that the flight down was exhausting and ask him if there isn't a better way to get here. Maybe ruby slippers.

Over the next few days, I swim and walk down the main street, checking in with people I know.

During the second week of my three-week getaway, Leila flies down from New York City and I pick her up in my rented car at the airport that is just two minutes from my apartment. We swim, she drives the rental car, we go out to dinner at the Slipway where I close my eyes as she expertly drives down the impossibly curvy road on the steep hill to the seaside restaurant.

She brings me a Christmas present—a jigsaw puzzle about women who've made a difference. We spill the pieces out on the balcony table and start. I grab for the cover with the photo on it.

"Nana, you can't do that. It's cheating."

So I put it away and we work on it together, piece by piece, Rosa Parks, Marie Curie, Ella Fitzgerald, Harriet Tubman, until it's finished. She's great company and I'm so grateful her work schedule allowed her to come down. We have Nellie and her daughter and brother to dinner. We make a chicken curry and the delicious bananas flambé. Nellie's teen-aged daughter, Daja, was born here in Carriacou but had never eaten bananas flambé. She loves it.

I ask Nellie about Ms. Massima, the old woman who celebrated her one hundred and eighteenth birthday last fall with a big party. I've seen pictures of her on Facebook and the look on her face is ecstatic about all the love she's being shown and the number of people who have come to her party.

"I know her," Nellie says. "I visit all the time. Would you like to meet her?"

"I'd love to," I say.

"I'll set it up and call you tomorrow," Nellie says.

Nellie says she is traveling to New York in August and might be able to come to Maine for a visit. She and Leila exchange contact information before they leave. Leila packs her bags. I'm sad to see her go. The next morning she flies to Grenada in the six-seater to catch her plane back to New York.

That leaves me alone. Everywhere I go, people say, "How's your husband?" "Where's Mr. Bill?" Joy who runs the Hardwood Bar, my friend Clemencia who is the curator of the little museum, Lydia, Nellie, Rina, Endeave, the man who raises sheep in Windward—they all loved Bill, too. Many people knew because of Facebook but some hadn't heard the news. All of them almost collapsed when I told them Bill had been in a bad accident and died. Their sorrow is heartfelt. No one here asks how I'm doing. They all know that it's damned hard but it's all part of life.

Leila sends an email just before boarding the flight from Grenada to New York. "I had a wonderful time! Good luck with the rest of your trip! Break down!!! Boarding!" I wasn't quite sure what the "Break down" was about.

The day after Leila leaves, Nellie takes me to see Ms. Massima. Nellie said she loves to have company. We drive up a steep dirt road and enter her humble home, where her 85-year-old daughter cares for her. 118 years old. It's hard to believe anyone could be that old. Nellie and I walk through the dim hallway to the clean but sparse bedroom where she's resting. There's a commode next to the bed, which means she must get out of bed to use it. She is small and dark, almost hidden by a sheet. The room is dim, cozy, comfortable.

Nellie gently helps her sit up. "Mama, someone is here to see you. A nice lady from the U.S." Ms. Massima extends her hand, and although she is blind, her eyes look directly into mine and my eyes look directly into hers, as if I were looking through a tear in the heavens. She holds my hand and we talk back and forth for over ten minutes, alert as anyone I know although she doesn't see and her hearing isn't great.

"Thank you for coming to visit me," she says.

"It's an honor," I say, but she doesn't reply. I don't think she hears me.

"You come back next time?"

"Yes. Yes I will," I say. And this time she nods.

Nellie speaks close to her ear so she can understand. "Mama, how have you been?" Nellie asks.

"Not too bad," Ms. Massima says.

"You had a great party on your birthday," I say.

"Yes," Ms. Massima says. "A wonderful time. So many people."

"Did you sit on the porch today?" I ask.

"Every day," she says in her clear voice. "Thank you," she says when Nellie helps her lie back down and we get ready to leave.

"Thank you, Ms. Massima, for welcoming me into your home."

"I won't see you again before you go," she says.

"No. But I will come back next year, when you are a hundred and nineteen."

She smiles back at me, as if she sees my smile. But I think she heard me this time.

Outside, I become weepy. "I've just looked into the face of God," I say to Nellie. "Not really, but that's how I feel. Thank you for bringing me to see her."

Something about visiting with her moves me, opens up something inside me. She's lived thirty-five years more than Bill already and she's still alert and aware. Life is such a great thing but you never know how long you're going to have it. Some people die young. Some live long healthy lives. Some live long, desperate, and miserable lives. It's often what you make of it but mostly it's the luck of the draw.

The next day, while I'm swimming in the jade blue ocean right in front of my place, I can see far down the beach on both sides and there's no one swimming or walking. Just endless sand. Small shore birds play in the surf and pelicans dive for fish. The pelicans chase schools of little minnows and scoop them up. I can tell where the minnows are by the look of the surface of the water.

I feel Bill everywhere but nowhere. I dive deep and bring up a small piece of hard pink coral shaped like a Y. It feels rough in my hand. I let it fall back into the water. The water is so clear I can watch it drift slowly back and forth toward the sand below. That's the answer. I dive down again and pull up a smooth, round stone this time, drop it back into the water and watch as it settles back into the sand faster than the piece of coral. That's the way of the world, *n'est pas?* It's the rhythm of birth and death, of living as good a life as you can. It's to be honest with ourselves about what life is and what we should do with it. And you can't ever know how long that life will be or what will destroy it.

I look across at the island called Jack Adan, which has always fascinated me. About a mile out, it used to be a leper colony and is now uninhabited. I stare at the island and imagine the people living there away from others, lesions covering their skin, I wonder if they had lovers or children and if their parents ever visited. They closed the colony when modern medicine discovered antibiotics could cure the malady. No one has lived on Jack Adan for many years.

My tears spill down my face into the sea. For the lepers? For some reason, I feel desperate. I say aloud, "Are you out there Bill? Are you? Bill?"

I swim quite a ways out toward the little island until I'm exhausted. Years ago I could easily have swum all the way out but now I'm too old.

"Bill, I know you're not out there. Are you?" I sob for the lepers and for the loss of Bill. That's what Leila meant. She knew I needed to shake off everything and break down. And it took an old woman and ghosts of lepers abandoned on an island to bring me to a place where I could open myself up to my grief.

I know I'm not going to find him. He's gone and the body that served us both well for years is decaying in a box back at the farm. I think of the piece of coral and the round stone that I pulled up from the bottom of the sea and then dropped back down from whence they came. That's the way it works. The world. It's like the tide. In and out, in and out. Sometimes it's rough and sometimes it's gentle. Sometimes it's a big tide. Sometimes not. But it still goes in and out. And it feels good to be part of the main scheme of things.

"I know where you are, Bill. Your body's beginning the process of going back to dust. And that's the way it should be." I make the sign for "I love you," with my hand out of the water towards Jack Adan. I hold my arm up as long as I can, until it aches. Whatever love means, I feel it for the lepers of the past and the present, for an old woman who has lived a very long time, and for Bill, my friend, my lover, "Buppa," "Dad," my silly husband who never once told me what to do. And that means letting it all go. And I'm doing it. I'm letting it go, but holding on to the memories of all the fun we had together.

And I begin to laugh thinking of some of the great times we had. I laugh and cry at the same time. It's cathartic. Leila knew if I let my guard down it would happen. I dive down into the sea, just to invigorate my face. When I come up for air, I shake my head, gaze out at Jack Adan one more time.

And through my tears and the splashes of the whitecaps, I imagine a hand extended toward me, just imagine it, giving a small wave, like Mainers and Kayaks do, just a small gesture, and then it drops back into the ocean.

Elegy

"I Did What I Could"
Shepsi's song for Bill

When I first came to this land
I was not a farmer man
So I got myself a farm
And I did what I could

Started clearin' land with ponies three
Tilled up a garden so we could eat
These carrots taste so good to me

And the land was sweet and good
And I did what I could

When I first came to this land
I was not a loggin' man
So I got myself a horse
And I did what I could

Jack he twitched the logs to the yard
We piled the pulpwood high in the cart
Stefan and Gus they pulled it home
Andy and Star are the dreams I've known

And the land was sweet and good
And I did what I could

When I first came to this land
I was not a milling man
So I got myself a saw
And I did what I could

Started millin' boards for a new farm store
There would be a wool shed section
In '95 we had an erection

And the land was sweet and good
And I did what I could

When I first came to this land
I was not a political man
So I joined a board or two
And I did what I could

They asked who is this hippie man
Bearded, naked, with dirty hands
Why does a barnyard smell like his boots
He loves to watch the Highlands screw

And the land was sweet and good
And I did what I could

When I first came to this land
I was not a fertile man
So I got a New Idea
And I did what I could

I started with a pile of poop
Loaded up the spreader scoop by scoop
I've got the horses on the lines
I love to see that kaka fly
Smiling in my funny hat

And the land was sweet and good
And I did what I could

When I first came to this land
I was not yet Farmer Bill
So I got myself some land
And I did what I could

And we called the land Darthia Farm

And the land was sweet and good
And I did what I could

And I'll do what I can
And we'll do what we can.

Acknowledgments

Thank you to all the caring people who helped with the events in this book and enabled me to write with clarity and truth.

Thanks to my wonderful and insightful editors, interns, and artists at Islandport Press, Dean Lunt, Shannon Butler, Katherine Berube, Piper Wilbur, and Emily Lunt.

To my astute and talented editor, Fran Hodgkins, who has been a joy to work with.

Our children, Tom Saad and partner Riley Dalton, Sara Goldberg and partner Dwane Christian, and Amy Carlson. Our grandchildren, Leila and Brianna Saad, Sinai Herrera, Ruby Taddeo, and Eric Goldberg.

Our dear friends and relatives, Art and Becky O'Keefe, Wendy Gignoux, Colleen Wallace, Mary Laury, Cathy Johnson, Lisa Underwood, Don Sinclair, Jeff Beckley, Tom and Susan Duprey, Shepsi Eaton, Liz Moran, Sepp Huber, Sheila Unvala.

Members of my writing group, Jeff Jeude, Susan Dewey, Durin Chappe, Roy Gott, Sherry Christie. Also members of my first writing group who listened to my fiction over the years, Annaliese Jakimides, Brian Dyer Stewart, Mel Rice Schoon, and Kristen Britain.

Many thanks to my readers, Wendy Gignoux, my first agent, Sandy Choron, Becky O'Keefe and Art O'Keefe.

To my dear friend and fellow writer, Susan Hand Shetterly, for reading and commenting when I asked her to.

To my parents, who instilled in me the love of music and books.

To Lettie Bruce-Williams who taught me how to care for and ride horses and showed me other ways to live in the world.

And especially to our entire community; Schoodic Arts for All, Gouldsboro EMTs and fire department, the selectboard and town of Gouldsboro, the Wednesday Spinners, the Schoodic Summer Chorus, Meetinghouse Theatre Lab, and the nurses and doctors of Eastern Maine Hospital, who came together to show their support in so many ways.

About the Author

Cynthia Underwood Thayer was born in New York City and grew up in Nova Scotia. She received her BA and MA in British Literature at Bridgewater State University before moving to Maine with her husband in 1976. She has lived on Darthia Farm since then and is an expert in growing, dyeing, and spinning wool as well as in farm-to-table gourmet cooking. Thayer has previously written three novels—*Strong for Potatoes*, *A Certain Slant of Light*, and *A Brief Lunacy*. For more information visit cynthiaunderwoodthayer.com.